The Myth / Truth of God Incarnate

John Macquarrie   Michael Marshall

Jon Sobrino   Dennis Nineham

Don Cupitt   Roy Sano

Richard Norris

The Tenth National Conference of Trinity Institute

The Myth/Truth
of God Incarnate

The Myth/Truth of God Incarnate

The Tenth National Conference
of Trinity Institute

Durstan R McDonald, Editor

Morehouse-Barlow Co., Inc.
Wilton, Connecticut

Other Books From Trinity Institute

The Future of the Christian Church

by Arthur Michael Ramsey
Leon-Joseph Suenens

The Charismatic Christ

by Arthur Michael Ramsey
Robert E. Terwilliger
A. MacDonald Allchin

Come Holy Spirit

by Arthur Michael Ramsey
Robert E. Terwilliger

MOREHOUSE-BARLOW CO., INC.
78 Danbury Road, Wilton, CT 06897

ISBN — 0-8192-1266-0

Printed in the United States of America

Contents

v

Preface

The person of Jesus is central to the Christian faith. Historically, belief in the Incarnation — that is, the assumption of full humanity by the Son of God or the full divinity of the human Jesus — has been essential to Christianity. In the past, believers and unbelievers agreed that belief in the Incarnation is essential to Christian faith. Now, however, some Christian theologians have suggested that the conception of Jesus as God incarnate is a mythological or poetic way of expressing his significance for us.

Although many of the positions expressed in this volume sound surprisingly new and novel, they are neither. The nineteenth-century antecedents are obvious and the varying Christologies, orthodox and unorthodox, are the Christologies of clergy and lay people throughout the church. To understand that this is so is not to give consent, but to see the importance of thinking the matter through more carefully.

This conference appropriately reflects the wide range of interpretation of a central tenet of the Christian Church: the doctrine of the Incarnation. The diversity of theological opinion surfaced publicly in the volume of essays, *The Myth of God Incarnate*, which was countered by a collection of defenses of orthodox Christian doctrine entitled *The Truth of God Incarnate*. The titles are unfortunate in their use of *myth* and *truth* as antithetical terms. Contrary to popular usage, the deepest truths that we hold to be self-evident are myths. In the United States we believe in the dignity and equality of individuals, freedom of the press and religion, the desirability of a minimum standard of living, the primacy of the Constitution and the law over officials of our government, et al. Many other cultures in other places or other times do not share these beliefs. The question is not that of myth versus truth but what are the myths that we will live by? What are we to say of this Jesus whom we call Lord?

Honesty compels us to begin with the recognition of the distance of the world of the disciples of Jesus and the authors of the New Testament from our world and our thoughts. True, the point was made long ago by scholars like Harnack and Bultmann, but the problem remains all too often buried rather than acknowledged. The ministry of Jesus is consistently portrayed in Scripture as a teaching ministry heralding the advent of the Kingdom of God and a healing ministry exercising power over demons. Only when the strangeness of that ministry and the worldview of the first century is faced honestly can we begin to answer the question of who Jesus is for us today.

While there must be an acknowledgement of the differences of what separates us from the world of the New Testament, it is also necessary to insist on what we have in common. The doctrine of the Incarnation has signified different aspects of the revelation of God in Christ to different ages and cultures. It also signifies different truths to each of us at different times in our lives. But still the doctrine of the Incarnation, however understood, presents a constant challenge to conceptual categories. To speak of the divinity and humanity of Jesus is to allow our ideas of God to be drastically changed by what we learn about God and humanity through Jesus Christ. Contrary to our natural religious inclination to think of God in terms of power, any notion of the divinity of Christ impels us to think of God primarily in terms of love and vulnerability. What is at stake in the doctrine of the Incarnation is what we are to say about God and about human life on the deepest level.

There is both continuity and discontinuity in the church's teaching about the Incarnation. If we seriously try to understand our experience and lives in the twentieth century in the light of the commitment involved in affirming God's incarnation in Christ, two things will happen: We will begin to see Jesus in new ways and we will begin to see our life and our world in new ways. We must always engage in rethinking our understanding of the mystery of the manifestation of God in Christ, just as we must allow that revelation to shed new light on how the contemporary world appears to us.

The sharpest critique of the myth/truth debate comes from those theologians, loosely called "liberation theologians," who locate true knowledge of Jesus as Lord in the living out of Christian discipleship. Recovering an urgent sense of the message of Jesus of the coming Kingdom of God, Jon Sabrino and Roy Sano press for a movement beyond conceptual formulations of an academic theology. Essential to any real knowledge of Jesus as Lord, any adequate Christology, is engagement in the praxis of building the Kingdom of God.

Two features of the debate about Jesus Christ — one a major omission and the other a surprising note of agreement — require some attention. Missing is any real discussion of the resurrection of Christ. Ours is an Easter faith. Jesus is called Lord and God by Thomas after the Resurrection. What Jesus did is normative for who we say he is. Any Christology which is not rooted in the Crucifixion/Resurrection will not adequately reflect the event and the person who shattered and transformed the accepted use of the terms *God* and *Messiah*.

Disturbing as this omission is, the agreement of our writers on the importance of Christian discipleship is even more striking. Whatever each writer is affirming or denying about the Incarnation, each is concerned with salvation, life in the Kingdom of God, and the response of the believer to God as manifested in the human person of Jesus. Just as Cupitt emphasizes the call of Jesus to a new life, Marshall and Nineham both stress the new relationship with God in the Christian community, Macquarrie and Norris the realization of the potentialities of our humanity, Sano and Sobrino the following of Christ in solidarity with the outcast and dispossessed of our own culture. Here we enter the central concerns of our faith, as it is written: "Not everyone who says to me 'Lord, Lord' will enter the kingdom of heaven, but he who does the will of my Father who is in heaven."

Holy Cross Day, 1979   *Durstan R McDonald x*

The Jesus of Faith and the Christ of History

Don Cupitt

According to standard Christian doctrine, there are within God three distinct, coequal and coeternal persons: the Father, the Son and the Holy Spirit. In the fullness of time, the second of these persons — God's eternal Son — took human nature in the womb of Mary, a woman of first-century Galilee, and appeared among men as Jesus of Nazareth. The incarnate Lord, Jesus Christ, is a being fully divine and fully human.

As is well known, this doctrine of the true status of Jesus was not defined until three or four hundred years after his death, and even then only after bitter controversies. In 451, however, when the Council of Chalcedon had fixed the doctrine, it declared that the doctrine had been taught by Jesus himself and believed ever since. To this day, most Christians accept that claim and regard the divinity of Christ as the most central and distinctive of all Christian affirmations. Church doctrine, art and liturgy present the life of Jesus as a grand pageant of revelatory events, teaching the tenets of the developed faith. The picture of Jesus thus presented in the cycle of feasts highlights his supernatural status and powers in order to show him as an unmistakably superhuman figure.

A series of traditional arguments for the divinity of Christ adheres to this view of Jesus. Each argument claims that he had some characteristic which no ordinary man could have, a characteristic from which we can infer that he is God incarnate. The qualities appealed to in this way include his fulfillment of prophecy, the performance of great miracles in and by him, his sinlessness, the authority with which he spoke, the excellence of his moral teaching, the greatness of his claims for himself and his performance of divine functions such as forgiveness, revelation and salvation. All these qualities and more were held to reveal his divine nature, which is attested to by all the New Testament writers.

In the nineteenth century, however, the new methods of critical historical research began to be applied to the origins and development of Christianity; the results were traumatic. The image of the divine Christ presented by the church came to be seen as the product of a long historical development and as a piece of church ideology. It had evolved a very long way from the original Jesus who, by the end of the nineteenth century, was emerging as a first-century Jewish teacher, healer, prophet and man of God. His message had been strongly eschatological, for he expected the end of history to arrive very soon. His followers believed him to be the Messiah. The titles they had given him — Lord, Christ, and Son of God — had originally been messianic rather than divine in meaning. It became clear that the classic Christian claims about Jesus were unfounded. There was no evidence that he had claimed divinity and it was unthinkable that his first followers believed him to be God. The shades of linguistic meaning are so fine that even today it is still hard to pin down just when the belief in his divinity arose; but, at any rate, it is certainly not original.

Jesus had little interest in Gentiles, or in founding a church. The later Gentile church liked to see him as the founder who had taught its doctrines, commissioned its ministry and instituted its sacraments; but all this was an anachronism. Jesus himself had not expected the Church, but the Kingdom of God. His actions and his teaching had all been dominated by the expectation that the end of all things, the Parousia, would arrive within a generation or so. The whole history of what we call Christianity as a distinct religion — the Gentile Church with its divine Christ — has arisen as a byproduct of the disappointment of that original hope. The faith of the Gentile Church was very different from the faith of Jesus and the first generation of believers.

This position was reached three generations ago and still remains substantially true. There could hardly have been a more comprehensive challenge to the developed faith of the modern Christian churches. Their doctrine of Christ was crumbling at every point.

We must admit the question of miracles and the supernatural. There has been a long history of rationalist philosophical criticism of miracles and some of the arguments this criticism has produced are very strong. It was argued that (a) miracles cannot happen, (b) that we can never have sufficient evidence to make it reasonable to believe that they have happened, (c) that there is some natural explanation of the supposedly miraculous event or (d) that the mythopoeic imagination of simple people has generated the stories. Such arguments did not make much impression on the churches, for people could always reply that, in the unique case of the Incarnation, one may expect ordinary rules to be broken and extraordinary things to happen. Modern criticism, however, points to a view of the Gospel miracles that is much more difficult to answer. First, it points out that historical research cannot cope with miracles because the ordinary rules of evidence cannot be applied to them. Secondly, it says that, in any case, a detailed literary explanation of why the stories were included in the narrative and how they have been developed can be given. So the question of historicity need not arise. It is probably true that Jesus was a healer, like many others of his day. But the supernatural events surrounding the beginning and end of his life and the great nature-miracles have all been developed from Old Testament sources by standard Jewish storymaking techniques and for theological reasons.

Second, we must admit that the traditional arguments from facts about Jesus to his divinity have all broken down. Either the premise is historically uncertain or the theology of the Gospel writers has been misunderstood and the inference is invalid. All the supernatural qualities of Jesus are borrowed from Old Testament characters such as Moses and Elijah and were attributed to him by the Evangelists with the object of showing him to be the last and greatest of the biblical men of God. They show not Jesus' divinity, but rather that he fulfills Scripture.

In the case of the Transfiguration, for example, a traditional preacher thought that this event really happened and that it showed Jesus' divinity. But a modern Gospel commentator has a quite different approach. He says that the Evangelist saw Jesus as the fulfillment of Scripture and the bringer of final salvation. Scripture tells how Moses' face shone on Sinai after he spoke with God; it promises a new Moses and a returned Elijah at the end of history. Thus the Evangelist's story of Jesus appearing on a mountain of revelation with a shining face and the support of Moses and Elijah. The story is not history but theology; it reveals Jesus not as divine, but as the eschatological deliverer promised in the Old Testament — a human figure.

Similar things have to be said about the rest of the standard arguments for Jesus' divinity. By the late nineteenth century it was established that St. John's Gospel must be set aside, Jesus did not speak like that. Matthew, Mark and Luke give a portrait of Jesus closer to history, but even they must be read with great caution. It became clear that Jesus had not claimed to be God and was even very hesitant about the title of Messiah. The old argument from his claims collapsed. His fulfillment of prophecy, his authority and the excellence of his moral teaching clearly do not prove his divinity. When he dispensed forgiveness he did not say, "I, being God, forgive you," but, "Your sins are forgiven (i.e., by God)," and he is presented as passing on the power of binding and loosing to his human followers. As for his supposedly unique filial consciousness of God, this was an attribute borrowed from the Israelite King. It had been part of the original Davidic Covenant that the King was God's Son. In Psalm 2, God says to the Israelite King, "Thou art my Son; this day have I begotten thee," and in the Greek version of that Psalm the King is called Christ. In Psalm 110, the King of Israel is a Lord exalted to sit at the right hand of God. Jesus' sonship and his messiahship are much the same thing and, by teaching his followers to pray "Our Father," he insisted that they should pray not to him, but with him to the God who is their Father as well as his.

Throughout the Gospels the authors were concerned to embed Jesus firmly in the tradition of Old Testament faith and hope, which of course included no idea of incarnation. The whole of their argument shows him as a human figure with a uniquely divine mission and endowed with God-given graces and powers. The earliest faith was not that Jesus is God, but that Jesus is Christ or Messiah, the eschatological deliverer.

Third, then, we must admit that the traditional titles of Jesus are not divine titles. When the Apostles' Creed summarizes the New Testament faith by speaking of "Jesus Christ God's only Son our Lord," it does not commit itself on the question of Jesus' divinity. The titles certainly mean that Jesus has been appointed by God to bring in and reign over the time of final salvation, but they need mean no more than that. Later doctrine declared that the Son of God is God of God, so that the phrase "Son of God incarnate" means, in effect, "God incarnate." But the New Testament never says that the expression, "Son of God," is equivalent in meaning to "God." Sonship means service, obedience, a task. The influence of later doctrine leads us systematically to misread the New Testament and see in it things which are not there at all. Most Christians think the New Testament teaches the doctrine of the Incarnation, but when we look closely we have to qualify that statement so much that little is left of it. The Son of God never quite becomes God the Son.

When the message and character of the real Jesus began to re-emerge at the end of the nineteenth century, the gap that struck people most forcibly was that between the Jesus of history and the Christ of faith. The historical Jesus had been a prophet of the Kingdom of God who was simply mistaken in his expectations. He had had no idea that one day there would arise a new religion based on him. Christian doctrine had lost its historical underpinning in the life of Jesus. It had arisen in the post-Easter Church. The leading theologians were, however, determined to save Christian doctrine, even without Jesus. So they said that Christianity began only after Jesus' death, when God retrospectively revealed the central beliefs about Jesus the Christ to the early church. On this view the Christian gospel and way to salvation were not available during Jesus' lifetime. The life and teaching of the historical Jesus were not in themselves of any special interest to Christianity and, in any case, were historically very hard to reach. The real nucleus of Christianity is the primitive Christian gospel. In effect, the historical Jesus is nothing, the christological beliefs are everything.

This so-called "neo-orthodox" theology was very popular between 1920 and 1960. It held that Christianity is not about the Jesus of history, but about the Christ of faith. Christianity became a set of dogmatic claims with little historical basis beyond an allusion to Jesus' death and resurrection as the peg on which God has hung the gospel of salvation by faith. The Incarnation was affirmed not as an explanation of Jesus, but as pure revealed dogma.

Because it was preoccupied with the problem of the Jesus of history and the Christ of faith, neo-orthodoxy tended to gloss over the gap between the primitive faith and the later fully-developed faith. It talked as if people like St. Paul had taught fully orthodox Christianity. But, with further study, we have come to see that that will not do. There are many Christs of faith and there is very considerable doctrinal development between the primitive faith of the first generation or two after Jesus' death and the more developed faith of later times.

Fourth, it has become uncertain how far the New Testament really teaches Jesus' divinity. The classic case is the theology of St. Paul, which I consider Jewish-Christian rather than orthodox. Paul's most noticeable doctrinal innovation is the preexistence of Christ. The idea begins to emerge in his letter to the Galatians: "When the time had fully come, God sent forth his Son, born of woman, born under the law, to redeem those who were under the law, so that we might receive adoption as sons."

Prophets had always been thought of as "sent" from God and as having been predestined by God in their vocation. Jesus is the last and greatest of the line. As the bringer of God's salvation and the final fulfillment of all things, he must have been in God's mind or at God's side from the beginning. Besides, in Paul's later letters the hope of the Parousia is already fading a little and he is beginning to think of Jesus' enthronement in heaven as more or less permanent. As God's permanent heavenly executive, Jesus is beginning to be talked of as rather like God's Wisdom.

In the religious imagination of late ancient Judaism, there were several ideas on a heavenly companion of God. This companion might be called the Word, the Wisdom, the Power or the Son of God. It was called God's image, because it was seen as the perfect created reflection of God. It was the first of all created things, the first-born; and, since man was also made in God's image, it might be identified with the Heavenly Man of the rabbis. Thus Philo of Alexandria had spoken of the *logos* as a heavenly Man.

This being cannot have been regarded as a second coequal person of God. There were no distinct persons in the one God of Jewish theology and the rabbis would not allow it to be said that there were two creators or two distinct foci of divine power and authority.

When Paul came to speak of Jesus as semipermanently enthroned in heaven and as preexistent, he borrowed the language used in speaking of this heavenly being. But preexistence is not necessarily divinity and God's sending of his son is not what would later be called the Incarnation. Paul's Jesus is an exalted heavenly Man. Paul regards Jesus as reigning over creation as Lord, Messiah and Son of God, seated at God's right hand. Jesus is the new Adam, God's perfect image in the created order, and the archetype of a new, redeemed and glorified humanity. But, like every New Testament writer, Paul uses the word *God* to mean God the Father, the God of Israel. He always carefully distinguishes Jesus from God and subordinates Jesus to God. For him, Jesus seems to be a creature, a preexistent heavenly being, closest to God and chief of all but, nonetheless, a creature.

A passage from Colossians is often cited as exemplifying the highest flight of the Pauline understanding of Jesus: "He is the image of the invisible God, the firstborn of all creatures." For Paul, Jesus is filled with God's spirit, laden with divine honors and functions and spoken of in close association with God. But all of these dignities are given to Jesus by God, not possessed by Jesus by nature and in his own right. Jesus does not bear witness to himself; God bears witness to him. Jesus does not raise, vindicate or exalt himself; God raises, vindicates and exalts him. Jesus owes everything to God. There is no suggestion that Jesus is by nature and by right a second divine Person equal to God the Father. Paul's theology is Jewish-Christian and says something quite different. In Paul's theology, the Lord Jesus Christ is everything that the creature is eternally meant to be: perfectly obedient and responsive to God, united with God, filled with God's spirit, exalted and eternally glorified by God. He is the peak of creation in its union with the Creator and he manifests the Creator's glory. But he is not himself the Creator. Jesus' relation to God is always one of dependence, instrumentality or representation and never one of identity or coequality. Jesus, in short, is not God but the Son of God.

As a brief summary of Christian faith and the Christian way to salvation, Paul uses the formula, "The Father, the Son and the Holy Spirit." Since Christians are deeply imbued with the later orthodoxy, they like to see the doctrine of the Trinity in this phrase. But there is no Trinity in the New Testament. What Paul speaks of is the union of God's Man with God by God's spirit, as a summary symbol of his vision of the redemption of the whole universe through Christ. Salvation is to be united with God by God's spirit in the way that Jesus has introduced. The phrase "the Son" stands not for a second coequal divine person, but for Jesus first and, through him, for every other creature which is to share his exaltation and his glory.

Obviously, much in Paul's theology is highly mythologial and alien to us. This applies especially to his idea of the preexistence of Christ. If we can make the effort to set aside later ideas and see him in his own right, however, it will be revelation. We will see that there was a primitive faith which was Jewish and eschatological in its categories, like Jesus himself, and was distinctly different from later orthodoxy.

We have reviewed four main areas in which the orthodox doctrine of the divinity of Christ has broken down: (a) the whole supernatural apparatus of the Gospels can no longer be regarded as historical. It is theology added by the Evangelists to show Jesus as the fulfillment of Scripture; (b) the traditional arguments for Jesus' divinity now appear obviously unsound; (c) the traditional titles of Jesus do not strictly imply his divinity; and (d) the earliest Christians did not believe in Jesus' divinity.

At this point, people refer to the four or five texts in the last New Testament writings — John's Gospel and the Pastoral

Epistles — where Jesus is designated "God." Even in those texts the meaning may not be that of the later orthodoxy. In Old Testament times it was possible to call a man "God" by virtue of the fact that God had endowed him with the fullness of divine authority. The King of Israel is called "God" in this sense in Psalm 45, in a text later to be taken up by the writer to the Hebrews. The king was certainly not thought of as literally divine; rather, he was divine in the same sort of sense as an ambassador is royal — by grace of appointment. It is permissible to treat an ambassador as standing for the sovereign he represents and to accord him royal honors, provided you remember that the ambassador is not a king in his own right. The ambassador is royal only by the king's grace and by his own fidelity to the terms of his commission. Similarly, the New Testament is occasionally willing, very cautiously, to call Jesus divine in virtue of the greatness of his commission from God and his human fidelity to his task. The New Testament does *not* say that Jesus is coequally and coeternally God of God by nature. Later orthodoxy advanced this concept, mistakenly I believe. In time, pious Christians spoke of Jesus in ways quite incompatible with the historical reality of Jesus and they developed a cult of Jesus' humanity which owes more to Greek humanism than to the Bible. We are all familiar with the modern idolatrous hero-cult of Jesus which is ludicrously false to the real Jesus and very nearly atheistic.

Among my friends and colleagues there are a number of theologians who broadly accept the aforementioned point of view. The question arises, then, which way should we go next? There are two possible answers. The first argues that, with the passage of the centuries, the original Jesus and the primitive Christian faith have now become so strange and remote that they can no longer determine the course of modern Christian life. In this respect, Albert Schweitzer rightly commented that Jesus and the first Christians held beliefs that we cannot possibly share and which, in any case, were mistaken. There is no stopping history and the process of cultural change. The Christian tradition is like a river, whose shape and course at any one time are determined by the shape of the ground over which it is flow-

ing. There may come a time when the church forgets Jesus altogether, except as the man who is dimly remembered as having
stood at the source of the river. The Church will have evolved so
far from him that there will no longer be any need for doctrines
on Jesus, for no sense will remain in which he is felt to be significant for the Church and to be influential in its life. There are a
few people who think we have already reached that point. They
think Christology is finished and that all we need are doctrines
of God, salvation and the Church which articulate the religious
experience of our own day.

I do not accept this view, mainly because I am so deeply at-
tracted by the choice of the historical Jesus and believe that his
voice is still of final religious importance to us, just *because* he
was such a strange eschatological prophet. The central religious
truth in Christianity is that the highest good of all — salvation —
can be had if one turns wholly to God in repentance and faith.
Jesus discovered this truth, the fulfillment of Israel's religious
quest, at his baptism. Turning wholly to God in repentance and
faith, leaving everything behind and making a wholly fresh start,
he received God's spirit and knew God's kingdom was a reality.

It was appropriate and fitting that he should cast his subsequent preaching in the language of eschatology. The death and
rebirth that he had discovered was not just individual, but
social; not just social, but cosmic in its implications. This way to
salvation was the repudiation of the old world and the reception
of a new world, the Kingdom of God.

We do not have any positively authentic sayings in his own
words, but the main outlines of Jesus' message, his tone of voice
and his distinctive linguistic techniques are recoverable. He used
language not to inform, but in a purely religious and practical
way, as a tool for producing an imaginative and moral change in
his hearer. One understands Jesus when his word breaks up an
old way of seeing oneself and the world and opens a new way,
the Kingdom of God. And just because his command is to die utterly to the old world, it is equally authoritative whatever world
one lives in. His apocalyptic finality *is* his universal authority,
because the command, "You must renounce the world and receive God's kingdom," is valid for all historical values of the ex-

pression "the world." Hence Jesus' voice and call is the gospel, the only part of Christianity which is cross-culturally constant. The human linguistic response to Jesus, in terms of doctrines, confessions of faith and the like, is not Gospel but Epistle. Inevitably, it is historically conditioned and variable.

I wish to reverse the value judgment made by the neo-orthodox theology. It regarded the historical Jesus as obsolete and claimed that the authoritative core of Christianity is the christological confession of the Church. I believe that position is indefensible. I claim that the voice and call of the historical Jesus — his call to God — is the permanent truth and the various Christs of faith are transient, historical products. Of them all, the most impressive and the closest to Jesus himself was the ardent eschatological faith of the first generation of believers. In union with them, I still speak of Jesus as Lord, Messiah and Son of God and, in union with the church, I pray to the One God through Jesus Christ our Lord. But to speak of him as coequal with God the Father is surely to lose touch with what he stood for. When the Gentiles at Lysta called them incarnations of Hermes and Zeus, Paul and Barnabas reacted in the traditional Jewish way, by tearing their clothes in horror. Is it not obvious that Jesus would have done the same? There is indeed an aura of divinity about Jesus and the word he speaks is a word of God; but the divinity that fills him is God the Father's and not his own.

The change of outlook that I am recommending shifts attention away from untenable ideas of unique, divine intervention and Jesus' metaphysical status and toward his work as the prophet and martyr who opens up a distinctive way to salvation. It may also help to heal the oldest and most damaging wound in the body of Christ, the split between Church and Synagogue. Since Jesus was no heretic or blasphemer but a mainstream Jew and the fulfillment of Scripture, Christianity has a deep historical obligation to express its faith in a way consistent with Jewish faith and values. I think it can be done and should be done.

The Humility of God

John Macquarrie

The title of this lecture, "The Humility of God," calls for some explanation. We usually think of God as the high and mighty One. How, then, can we think of him as humble?

There are, of course, many ways of thinking about God. Part of our trouble with the doctrine of incarnation is that we discuss the divinity and even the humanity of Christ in terms of ready-made ideas of God and man that we bring along with us, without allowing these ideas to be corrected and even drastically changed by what we learn about God and man in and through Jesus Christ. He, in fact, accomplished a revolution in the understanding of God. In place of the ancient gods of power, Christ preached a God who is to be understood as love before we think of him as power. That is why Karl Barth could say that it is as natural for God to be humble as to be great, why Dietrich Bonhoeffer could speak of God's coming among us in weakness, why Jurger Moltmann, in a startling exercise of the *communicatio idiomatum*, can write of the crucified God.

Allow me to remind you of a story which Søren Kierkegaard told which expresses both the myth and the truth of incarnation. The story begins like a fairy tale. There was once a noble king who loved a humble maiden. He lived in a palace, she in a tiny cottage. He was a powerful king, but also a very good king, and he was much troubled about what to do. If he went directly to the maiden and asked her to marry him, she might be so overwhelmed by the royal request that she would consent out of respect for his office. If he had a messenger go and speak to her on his behalf, he could imagine such a person saying, "The king is conferring a great honor on you and you should be grateful to him for the rest of your life!" This was not his idea of true love. Then he thought of disguising himself, of dressing up in old clothes and pretending to be poor. That would indeed have made it all a fairy tale! But there is no true love where there is deception, so there could be no disguise or pretense. There was only one way. The king must truly lay aside his power, rely on love alone, and become, not just in appearance but in reality, the equal of the humble maiden. As Kierkegaard said, "This is the unfathomable nature of love, that it desires equality with the beloved." Love implies humility and, if we accept that God is love, we are already well on the way to accepting a doctrine of incarnation.

Still, Kierkegaard was just as much aware as we are today of the difficulty of believing that there has lived on this earth a person we can call both God and man, a person in whom God has entered our history. Kierkegaard expressed the dilemma when he said that the Incarnation is "the absolute paradox." A paradox is not nonsense, but neither is it a straightforward empirical fact to be explained like the facts we encounter in everyday experience. In face of the paradox, Kierkegaard recommended what he called a "leap of faith." In the last resort, the claim we make for Jesus Christ is indeed a matter of faith, not of demonstration. We are, however, rational beings gifted by God with minds; it would be irresponsible if we made such a leap of faith — and, even more, urged others to make it — without having reflected as deeply as possible on the grounds for accepting such faith. Like most of the matters that concern us deeply in life, faith in Jesus Christ is not a question of proof, but of belief. We do not adopt beliefs, however, unless we have good grounds for thinking they are true and that they make sense.

I propose to deal with two difficult questions which trouble Christians today: How is it possible for one person to be truly God and truly man? Why do we claim Jesus Christ was that person? There can be no conclusive answers, but I hope that we can at least see a possible way through the difficulties and show that faith in Jesus Christ as the incarnate Word of God is a faith that makes sense and that can be held intelligently by people of our time.

How is it possible for one person to be truly God and truly man? Can we think of this paradox in such a way that we see that it is not nonsense, but points to a very profound truth? I don't think we can escape the paradox. Christianity would collapse if any lesser claim were made for Christ. Some have said he was truly God, not man; he only seemed to be a man, but was really a divine being who, so to speak, flitted across the stage of history in a human disguise. That view, held in the very early days of the church, is still I'm afraid how many people in the church think of Jesus. He is God, he is entirely elevated into the divine sphere. No matter how theologians protest, popular Christian belief does not take seriously the humanity of Christ. Perhaps this arises from a desire to honor Christ. But, in fact, it diminishes him. It makes him irrelevant to us for, if he did not share our humanity, he has nothing to say to us. Perhaps in exalting him we are unconsciously trying to remove him to a safe distance. If he gets too close, he makes us uncomfortable. If he is fully human, he exposes the shabbiness of our own humanity.

On the other hand, many people have acknowledged that Christ was truly man, but have denied that he was also in some sense God. Again, such people have been around from the earliest days of Christianity, but perhaps they are more common today when, although there has been a decline in belief in God, there is still a residual admiration for Jesus Christ. In the nineteenth century there was a so-called quest for the historical Jesus, an attempt to discover the purely human Jesus of Nazareth by digging down below all the mythological and theological accretions which have accumulated over the centuries. But a purely human Jesus could no more be the subject of a Gospel and could no more sustain the life and faith of the Christian church than could a purely divine Jesus. A purely human Jesus would remain (like many other figures of the past) as a great moral teacher or a great prophet and visionary, but he could not be the lord of history or have any final claim on our allegiance. He can only have that claim if there is about him an ultimacy; and this is what was meant in asserting his deity. When we claim that God was in Christ, we are asserting that he was more than just an exceptionally righteous man, though that would be a great deal. We are saying that in this man there has come to expression the ultimate reality that we call God, with his ultimate demand and his ultimate grace. If the Christian gospel continues to be proclaimed, there is no escape from this paradox of the one person who is truly divine and truly human. There is no deliverance from the problem of how a man can become the bearer of the divine or of how God can assume the nature of the human.

We may note that the doctrine of incarnation would be complete nonsense if God and man were two entirely different and alien natures. In that case, we would have not a paradox, but an impossibility. This might be true if one insisted so strongly on the transcendence (otherness) of God that there was really no way of relating him to the human. It is against any such view that I maintain what I am calling "the humility of God." The possibility of a God-man depends, on the one hand, on man's capacity for God and, on the other, a humanity in God himself.

Let us begin from the human side. How is it possible for a man, a human being (it could have been a woman, but we shall not go into that question), to be also, in some sense, God in the flesh? In approaching this question from the human side, we are following the general trend of contemporary theology. There is hardly a theologian today who does not begin his christological reflection from the humanity of Christ and, only when he has worked through that, does he begin to speak of Christ's deity. This is true of Roman Catholic theologians such as Karl Rahner, Anglicans such as John Knox and John Robinson and such great Protestant theologians as Wolfhart Pannenberg. There are many reasons for the contemporary determination to take the full humanity of Jesus Christ with new seriousness and to put it in the forefront of christological thinking.

First, there is the practical consideration that we live in a secular time when it is more difficult to talk of God than it was in earlier epochs. Therefore, just the practical demands of interpretation, preaching, and education will direct us to what might be called the low-key approach to the meaning of Jesus Christ. We must indeed be careful not to repeat the errors of the nineteenth-century quest or the errors of the various forms of adoptionism that characterized earlier centuries. But where can one begin to teach about Jesus Christ today if not with his humanity? Those who say that they are not interested in the question of God or that this question has no meaning for them are, nevertheless, interested in the question of humanity. What are its significance, its possibilities, its destiny? Jesus Christ is relevant to these questions. Yet even to begin one's teaching in this way is not merely a practical consideration, but also a theological one. The very idea of incarnation means meeting people where they are and, in a secular time, we do not meet them if we talk of God or the *logos* of the Trinity, but when we participate in their human problems.

Second, we must remember (but we often forget) that this was the route followed by the early disciples. They joined themselves to Jesus without, all at once, perceiving his full significance. They were drawn to him. At first, they thought of him as a rabbi, a charismatic prophet or a healer, certainly not as anything other than another human being. But as they kept company with him, as they learned more of the depth of his mind and spirit, as his mission and career unfolded, their understanding of him grew.

Finally, in answer to his question "Who do you say that I am?" Peter boldly replied, "You are the Christ!" At that stage (it may have been during his ministry, as the Gospels relate, or only after his resurrection, as many New Testament scholars suppose) they were still understanding the Christ as a purely human figure. As time went on and reflection continued, however, the disciples' estimate of Jesus deepened further. The story of the Transfiguration (whether it refers to a moment in the ministry or a post-resurrection appearance, and however it may have been originally understood) indicates a climactic moment in the disciples' growing understanding of Christ. He is transfigured before them, he shines like the sun, a voice attests his divine origin. There must have been some such moment in the disciples' experience when they perceived in Jesus Christ a new depth, a new "glory," to use the New Testament word. With this they are well on the way to the belief that he is not only fully and truly man, as they had always believed, but that in him we are meeting something of the glory of God. The story of the exploration of the meaning of

Christ did not end with the transfiguration or with the first generation of disciples, nor did it end with the Councils of Nicaea or Chalcedon. It is still going on today, for this Jesus in his ultimacy is inexhaustible.

How foolish it would be, then, to try to go back to the first dim guesses of those early disciples who were only beginning to open up the mystery, as if nothing of importance and no deeper spiritual insight occurred after their time! What a poor Christology that would confine itself to the few Jewish categories that were available then! It is as if someone were to show us an acorn rather than the growing, pulsating, majestic oak that grew out of it.

The disciples began with the human Jesus, but he continued to grow in depth in their understanding. We can still see something of this in the New Testament. The early preaching, represented by Peter's sermon on the feast of Pentecost, tells the story of a man who was crucified and then raised by God to be Christ and Lord. But soon another story was being told, the one we find in John's Gospel. It begins not with the human Jesus, but with the divine Word that dwelt with the Father in the beginning, came down to earth and was made flesh. The second story is undoubtedly the more profound of the two, for a man could not be raised to lordship and Christhood unless, in a very real sense, God had already descended into that man. The two stories are not rivals, however, and, likewise, adoptionism and incarnationism are not rivals. We need both stories, both conceptions, to do justice to the mystery of God in Christ. It is both the lifting up of man and the coming down of God.

Third, in the history of the church, that first story, the story of a man being raised to lordship and Christhood, has not maintained itself alongside the later story of the divine being who came down from heaven. It has been overshadowed by it and, if not quite forgotten, at least pushed very much into second place. The result has been, almost inevitably, to dim the true humanity of our Lord and to encourage that tendency, to which I drew attention earlier, to think of him in terms so exclusively divine that his humanity becomes unreal. It is not just in the last few years that this criticism has been made. As far back as the end of last century, Bishop Gore complained that "the general teaching about our Lord in the Catholic Church for many centuries has removed him very far from human sympathies."

The stress on the humanity of Christ, the demand that christological thinking should begin from a consideration of his humanity, is further justified when seen as a theological correction of the long-standing preoccupation with his deity. But it cannot be denied that, when a correction like this takes place, there is the danger of moving too far in the other direction. Corrections are often made in a clumsy heavy-handed fashion and, no doubt, some recent writers on Jesus, having jumped onto the humanistic bandwagon, are presenting us with such a thoroughly humanized Christ that they seem to have lost sight of the divine depth that came to expression in him and that gives him his ultimate significance for faith.

The risk of such errors must be endured, however, for the correction was long overdue. One can understand the impatient words of Pannenberg when he writes, "Where a statement that Jesus is God would contradict his real humanity, one would probably rather surrender the confession of his divinity than doubt that he was really a man." Of course, one is not finally driven to surrender either side of the christological paradox, and the gospel would be voided if Christ were anything less than truly God and truly man.

We must return now to the question of how such an idea is possible. At this point we receive a great deal of help from modern studies of the nature of humanity, which make it easier for us to see how there could be a divine humanity that was possible when older views of man prevailed. The great insight to be found in almost all modern understanding of man is that humanity is unfinished. It is still in the process of working out its own nature. For many centuries people talked about "human nature," but there is no fixed human nature. There is no universal essence that you can all "humanity," as there is a nature that belongs, let us say, to hydrogen or uranium. The human being is still in the process of forming its nature and, to some extent, is free to make its own nature through the deeds and decisions of life, whereas every other being on this earth is given its nature.

This insight is derived partly from the evolutionary theories which arose in the nineteenth century and replaced the idea of fixed species with a dynamic concept of development and coming to be. In the same century, Friedrich Nietzsche taught that man is a bridge, a stage on the way toward a form of being, the full nature of which still remains hidden. Nearer our own time, the existentionalists have taught that existence precedes man's essence; this means that he rises up in the world as a creative center who — admittedly, within limits — can decide what he will become. Even neo-Marxists — Herbert Marcuse, for example — have taken up this same idea, though in their terminology it is the word *transcendence* rather than *existence* which is used. The human individual and human society as a whole, they tell us, are in a process of constant transcendence, that is to say, moving out from any given state in which they find themselves into a new state. The new breed of Roman Catholic thinkers, such as Rahner and Bernard Lonergan, also use the concept of transcendence. They see human nature as open and, in particular, as open toward God, who is the goal of human transcendence. So man, although finite, has, in Friedrich Schleiermacher's famous phrase, "a sense and taste for the infinite." His very being is such that he keeps moving out from himself toward a horizon that recedes indefinitely.

Modern thinkers, then, see man as a being-on-the-way. Even if human nature, as we have so often known it in ourselves and others, is shabby, stunted and distorted by sin, it has an openness and possibility for transcendence. We can understand, then, that every human being has the potential for a fulfilled humanity, a true personhood, a coming to the point where this being of ours that is open toward God is, in fact, filled with the presence of God and begins to manifest his life. When we think in this way, we begin to glimpse something of what is meant by the idea of a man becoming the bearer of the divine.

Although I have been appealing here to modern views of man, the ideas are rooted in the Christian theological tradition. According to the Bible, man is made in the image of God and, however much it may be distorted, there is always the possibility of its coming to realization. This, according to the witness of the

New Testament, is what happened in the case of Jesus Christ. He is "the image of the invisible God" (Col. 1:15), "he reflects the glory of God and bears the very stamp of his nature" (Heb. 1:3). The possibility of expressing the divine nature so far as it can be expressed in the finite was realized in Christ. Some of the Greek fathers continued this dynamic understanding of man. They did not think that man had been created with a kind of readymade perfection (nothing is readymade in human existence). Man had to be forged in the course of experience and history. Thus, Theophilus of Antioch: "God gave man an opportunity for progress so that by growing and becoming mature and furthermore having been declared a god, he might also ascend heaven." The language here is partly mythological, but the understanding of man as an unfinished being on his way to an as yet undisclosed fulfillment of his nature is thoroughly modern. The idea that man might participate in and manifest the divine nature was common to many Greek fathers, notably Athanasius, and the idea even appears in a later book of the New Testament — 2 Peter — which speaks of Christians becoming partakers in the divine nature.

Beginning, then, from the humanity of Christ and seeing that humanity as the fulfillment of the imperfect humanity that we know in ourselves, we can affirm that in Christ the image of God has become explicit so that he is transfigured before us. We acknowledge that, in him, the divine nature is manifested in the world. We confess that "we have beheld his glory, glory as of the only Son from the Father" (John 1:14).

We have followed the way that leads upward from humanity to deity. Now we must consider the way that leads down, the way of descent from God to man. As I have already said, man could only rise to God if God had already descended into man; there can only be a deification of the human if there is already a humanity in God. It is the way from above down that has been traditionally stressed in speaking of Jesus Christ and, even if it has been allowed to overshadow the other story, it remains of fundamental importance because it recognizes God's initiative in this whole matter. It also recognizes that man, though he reaches toward the infinite, remains finite.

The belief that God has descended to us in Christ is best understood if we think of God (as we have also tried to think of man) in thoroughly dynamic terms. God is not, as I'm afraid so many Christians seem to think him, some static being dwelling in untroubled bliss apart from his creation, to be understood in terms of transcendence, majesty, power and the like. God is of a dynamic nature, involved in his creation, and, as such, constantly coming forth from himself in creative power. This is part of what we try to express in the doctrine of the Holy Trinity. God is a God of love and such a God does not remain shut up in his own perfections, but pours himself forth and finds joy in sharing the gift of existence with his creatures. This is what is meant when we say that, from the beginning, the Word was with God and the Word was God. A word is that which comes forth from someone and makes accessible what has hitherto been hidden in that person's mind. At the same time, a word is so close to the person who speaks it that it can rightly be regarded as an extension of that person. Christ as the incarnate Word has that kind of relation to the Father. In the traditional language, he is "one in being with" (*homoousios*) the Father.

The Christian understanding of God is that of a God coming out from himself and reaching beyond himself. The word expresses the Father and, through the Word, creation takes place. God, to some extent, is expressed in the whole creation, but obviously he is more fully expressed in some parts of it than in others. He is more fully expressed, for instance, in a person made to his image than in a fish or hydrogen atom. Thus God, in willing to express himself, chose the created work that would be able most fully to realize his purpose — a human being who would manifest the image of God in its fullness. It is in this sense that Barth ventured to speak of the humanity of God. He meant that the idea of man has always been present in the mind of God as that by which God intends to express himself, the reflection of God in the created order. So there has always been the possibility of incarnation. In fact, one might venture to say that, from the beginning, there has been the process of incarnation. For incarnation was not something that happened in a moment of time, it had been prepared for over the ages and, even in the life of Jesus, it was a process. This is part of what is hinted at through the idea of Christ's preexistence.

The idea of the God-man is a paradox, the absolute paradox, but I think we have seen that it is certainly neither nonsensical nor incoherent. It is in fact a profoundly reasonable idea. Given that there is a creative and loving God and a world like ours in which there has evolved man as a spiritual being made in the image of God, then it is by no means incredible that God — the loving author of this creation — wishing to establish the closest relation with it, has from all eternity willed to come into it himself in the only possible form in which he could express himself: in human form, so as to enter into that joyous personal communion with the creatures which, we believe, was the very goal of creation.

Incarnation, it is sometimes said, is a way of thinking conditioned by the culture of the first century, but incredible to people today. It belongs to the Hellenistic world, but not to ours. To some extent this is true; the titles applied to Jesus in the New Testament and the cosmological ideas belong to a vanished age. But the business of theology is to keep on refurbishing and reinterpreting these matters. As far as the central idea of incarnation is concerned, it is one of the most profound that has ever appeared in the history of religion. It is not surprising that in many non-Christian religions there is a tendency to develop incarnational beliefs. The mind is almost naturally led in such a direction if one believes that this world of ours is not a chance collection of atoms but has proceeded from a divine creative source.

Whereas we may have shown the strength of the idea of incarnation, we must still deal with the second question we posed: Why do we claim that this incarnation has taken place in Jesus Christ? Why do we believe that it was in this obscure figure of two thousand years ago that God became incarnate? Surely this is improbable in the highest degree.

Again, let us remember that such objections are not new. Even in the time of our Lord people were questioning his right to act or speak on matters that they considered too lofty for him. People in Nazareth contemptuously asked, "Is not this the car-

penter's son?" (Mt. 13:55). Surely God would not be so foolish
as to choose such a one as his messenger; it should have been a
high priest or a prince, or perhaps nowadays we would think
that at least an Oxbridge don would be required. But perhaps
God does act foolishly in human eyes. He turns all our standards
of judgment upside down for, as Paul said, "God chose what is
foolish in the world to shame the wise, God chose what is weak
in the world to shame the strong, God chose what is low and de-
spised in the world" (1 Cor. 1:27-8). The God of the Christian
religion is not some proud ruler exercising arbitrary power, like
the gods of the pre-Christian era. The God of the Christian religion turns all that upside down. That is why I venture to speak
of the humility of God. He is the God who comes among us in
weakness to stand with us in our suffering, as many modern
theologians have come to recognize, especially Barth, Bonhoeffer and Moltmann. Perhaps it will only seem incredible that God
should have revealed himself in the carpenter's son, the crucified
man, if we begin with a falsely conceived idea of God as a Louis
XIV of the heavens.

Why do we believe that, in a signal and definitive way, God
was incarnate in the particular person of Jesus Christ? What is so
special or unique about him that we make such a claim? I think
the first answer to this question can only be that the definitive
place of Jesus Christ is a given of history. This is the way things
have turned out. This man, however obscure his origins, has had
a unique influence on the spiritual life of mankind. And, as Hans
Küng has remarked, "Whatever the reason for it, the fact deserves careful consideration that this figure is obviously still for
innumerable people the most moving figure in the long history of
mankind." Now the skeptic may say that it was just one of the
accidents of history that the Christian religion, rather than one
of the many other cults that proliferated in the Hellenistic world,
seized the imagination of mankind and that the Christian cult
was just as illusory as the others. No one could prove the skeptic
wrong. The Christian will believe, however, that it was no acci-
dent but the providence of God that led some men and women to
see in Jesus Christ a glory that addressed them with an ultimacy
they had not found elsewhere.

Again, the New Testament writers were not wrong when they spoke of Christ coming in the fullness of time. In history, both the universal and the particular are blended together. All moments are not alike; some are pregnant with a meaning that lights up many others. When it is asked whether it is conceivable that God would have granted a universal knowledge of himself through this particular human being living at a particular time in a particular corner of the world, perhaps one can only reply with another question: "How else?"

Attempts have sometimes been made to say just precisely what it is in Jesus Christ that makes him the fulfillment of humanity and therefore the person who has become transparent to God. What gives him his definitive status? Is it his self-giving love, his capacity to live for others? Is it his freedom and his mastery of all situations? Is it his creativity, especially his creative influence on others? Is it his utter obedience to the Father, his unswerving integrity in his mission? Or is it his remarkable, almost self-authenticating moral authority?

Various theologians have drawn attention to one or the other of these characteristics, but I don't think that any one of them can be isolated or all the weight placed on any one of them. Many of them can, in fact, be paralleled in other great religious figures. But I think one can say that, in Jesus Christ, there is a concentration of what we recognize as the elements of a truly authentic human person — the fulfillment and also the transcendence of the unfinished, imperfect humanity that we know in ourselves and others — bringing it to a new level which we call God-manhood. This is also what we mean when we speak of his resurrection and think of him as the first fruits of a general resurrection. He has risen to participate in the divine nature, though indeed he has done so only because in him God has already descended into our humanity.

The Person of Christ in the Experience of the Church

Michael Marshall

There are three things I want to talk about today: first, my discontent over the strange plight of theology in the English-speaking world in recent years; second, how this has affected the contemporary debate on Christology; and third, the essential and minimal ingredients in any Christology which is still remotely capable of conveying "good news" and gospel to our world, while at the same time being faithful to the experience of the Church in its worship, prayer and ministry of reconciliation.

What, then, of my criticism of such theology? Kenneth Leech, in his book *Soul Friend,* writes:

> The gulf between academic theology and the exercise of pastoral care and spiritual guidance has been disastrous for all concerned. We are often told the gulf is exaggerated or that it does not exist at all, but these assurances are unconvincing. The study of theology, or at least of Christian Theology, cannot survive in a healthy state apart from the life of prayer and the search for holiness.

The theologian, then, is essentially and primarily a man of prayer, living in the environment of prayer and sharing with others his experience of prayer. Evagrius writes: "A theologian is one whose prayer is true: if you truly pray you are a theologian." Indeed, the entire tradition of the Eastern Church rejects totally what we might call "detached" theology. Kenneth Leech continues:

Theology is an encounter with the living God not an uncommitted academic exercise. This encounter cannot survive if its only locus is the lecture theatre or the library. It needs the nourishment of sacramental worship, of solitude, of pastoral care and the cure of souls. Theology must rise out of being constantly related to a living situation.

It was Anthony Bloom who said: "Theology is knowing God, not knowing about God, much less knowing what other people know about God." In this he is consistent with the whole Eastern tradition. Vladimir Lossky, in his book *The Mystical Theology of the Eastern Church,* writes:

There is no Christian mysticism without theology, but above all there is no theology without mysticism. It is an existential attitude which involves the whole man: there is no theology apart from experience: it is necessary to change and become a new man. To know God one must draw near to him. No one who does not follow the path of union with God can be a theologian. The way of the knowledge of God is necessarily the way of deification.

So Alexander Schmemann, in his recent book *Of Water and the Spirit,* speaks of the fateful divorce between theology, liturgy and piety,

. . .a divorce which especially in the West has had disasterous consequences for theology as well as for liturgy and piety. It deprives liturgy of its proper understanding by the people who begin to see in it beautiful and mysterious ceremonies in which while attending them they have no real part. It deprives theology of its living source and makes it into an intellectual exercise for intellectuals. It deprives piety of its living contant and terms of reference.

If you feel more at home, however, in our own Western tradition, then there is the reassurance of our own Karl Barth, when he writes in his *Evangelical Theology:* "Theological work does not merely begin with prayer, it is not merely accompanied by it: in its totality it is the peculiar characteristic of theology that it can be performed only in the act of prayer."

Now beware! I am not pleading for an anti-intellectual theology, but for a superintellectual theology and, furthermore, for a theology which is done in the environment of faith, prayer, worship and repentance. I do not want an apologetics which only speaks to experience and *bypasses* the intellect, but rather one which speaks to the whole man in an environment of faith which inevitably *surpasses* the intellect. "I believe in order that I may understand" is the cry of the apologetics of the Church throughout its history. Reinhold Neibuhr wrote: "Faith is the intellect in ecstasy." I think it was Malcolm Muggeridge who said that the trouble with this generation was that it has got sex on the brain and it was just about the worst place you can have it. *Mutatis mutandis,* dare I say that this generation of theologians has got theology on the brain and it's just about the worst place you can have it?

The environment in which theology in the English-speaking world is done is all too limited and the evidence upon which it draws is also all too limited. We cannot, in other words, ask the question — any more than it was asked when it was first enunciated — "Whom do men say that I am?" outside the context and environment of the church, its faith and discipleship and its experience of Christ in its worship and in its penitence, as well as in the words of Jesus as they are recorded in the New Testament. But I refer not only to the strange and clinical environment in which much contemporary theology is undertaken, but also to the limited evidences upon which it calls in the pursuit of its craft. Whoever pretended — except a kind of disappointed biblical fundamentalist — that you can arrive at the Chalcedonian definition of the person of Christ only from an analysis of the pages of the New Testament? There is something which both predates and presupposes that written record in the New Testament and something which, in the end, outdates that written record — i.e., the experience of the risen Christ within the band of his disciples. This is what predates any attempt by the writers of the New Testament to talk about Jesus or the Incarnation. They had experienced the dying and rising of Jesus and that alone was what gave significance not only to his words and his works in the years before the Crucifixion and Resurrection, but also in their understanding of his person and his origin. So Michael Ramsey can write:

> A few days before Christmas just when we are preparing to journey in mind to Bethlehem, the feast of St. Thomas the Apostle suddenly break upon us and we are confronted by the risen Jesus, the wounds of Calvary and the disciples' faith. That is the right order: that is how Christianity began. There was first the Easter faith and the preaching of the death and resurrection of the Messiah. From that root there grew the doctrine of the deity of him who died and rose again. From the Cross and Resurrection faith there grew the mature doctrine of the apostolic age, faith in the God who had given himself in Jesus and faith in Jesus himself went together as the theism and the Christology were interwoven. There grows that devotion to Jesus which would be idolatrous if it were not true.

The pages of the New Testament, then, are set within that environment and that experience and they do not make sense outside of it. Furthermore, the chronological definition of 451, although referring to the foundation documents of the New Testament, also draws upon 450 years of prayer, worship, the experience of forgiveness and healing and a personal knowledge, love of and incorporation into the person of Jesus who died and rose again. To believe that, out of context, the pages of the New Testament give us or, on the other hand, do not give us the Chalcedonian definition of his perosn is nothing less than biblical fundamentalism turned upside down. The context and the content belong together and not least when we are about that most difficult, yet central doctrine of Christianity — the person and nature of Christ. If I were to find in my wife's dressing-table drawer the picture of another man, I could begin a long and protracted (largely archeological and genetic) discussion about the aperture of the lens, the speed of the film and the make of the camera with which the photograph had been taken. I modestly suggest, however, that a more urgent and apposite question might arise in my mind. What is the relationship between that man and my wife now? I do not say that the archeological question may not at some point be important, but they derive their importance (or relevance) from the nature of the relationship and the quality of that relationship rather than any archeological discussion for its own sake about the occasion on which the photograph was taken. Likewise, any discussion on Christology must be set in a wider context than we find in much theology today, as well as in the collection of essays entitled *The Myth of God Incarnate* in particular.

I agree, of course, that in the pages of the New Testament there is a pluralism of Christologies. I would be suspicious if there were not. Unanimous evidence is generally rigged and any detective is rightly suspicious of it. However, there is no doubt in my mind that a crime has been committed in fact, in time and in space! Michael Ramsey says: "Christmas is about fact, or it is about nothing." I must agree that some explanations of it are better than others and that, at the end of the day, one is true and the others are false to a greater or lesser degree. C. S. Lewis writes:

> If any man is tempted to think — as one might be tempted if one read only contemporary theologians — that Christianity is a word of so many meanings that it means nothing at all he can learn beyond all doubt by stepping out of his own century, that this is not so. Measured against the ages "mere Christianity" turns out to be no insipid interdenominational transparency, but something positive, self-consistent, and inexhaustible. I know it, indeed, to my cost. In the days when I still hated Christianity, I learnt to recognise, like some all too familiar smell, that almost unvarying *something* which met me, now in Puritan Bunyan, now in Anglican Hooker, now in Thomist Dante. It was there (honeyed and floral) in Frances de Sales; it was there (grave and homely) in Spencer and Walton; it was there (grim but manful) in Pascal and Johnson; there again with a mild, frightening, paradisial flavour in Vaughan and Traherne. In the urban sobriety of the 18th century one was not safe — Law and Butler were two lions in the path: the supposed "paganism' of the Elizabethans could not keep it out; it lay in wait where a man might have supposed himself safest, in the very centre of the Faerie Queen and the Arcadia. It was of course, varied: and yet — after all — so unmistakenly the same: recognisable, not to be evaded, the odour which is death to us until we allow it to become life.

Although there is an inconsistency, there is an overwhelming consistency in mere Christianity which was Baxter's word for what some of us would want to call today's mainstream Christianity. It is of course true that there are many variations and a pluralism of Christology.

However, there are several things which need to be said about a pluralism of Christologies in criticism of some of the unquestioned assumptions which run throughout the writings of the book entitled *The Myth of God Incarnate*. These have been said remarkably well by Professor Charles Moule in his recent book *The Origin of Christology*. The first point is made conclusively by Professor Moule in his helpful distinction between the concept of "evolution" and the concept of "development" when we are talking about the history of Christological doctrine. He writes:

> I find my own reading of the evidence leading me to the view that development is a better analogy for the genesis of Christology than evolution. This is only an analogy of course; I am in no way concerned to deny evolution in the biological field. But if, in my analogy, "evolution" means the genesis of successive new species my mutations and natural selection along the way, "development," by contrast, will mean something more like the growth, from immaturity to maturity, of a single specimen from within itself. . . They are not successive additions of something new, but only the drawing out and articulating of what is there. They represent various stages in the development of perception, but they do not represent the accretion of any alien factors that were not inherent from the beginning: they are analogous not so much to the emergence of a new species, as to the unfolding (if you like) of flower from bud and the growth of fruit from flower.

Second, and I think this is very important indeed, Moule challenges us and tells us that we must not assume that early Christologies are "low" and later Christologies are "high." He writes:

> My point is that the evidence does not support the assumption that a "high" Christology evolved from a "low" Christology by a process of borrowing from extraneous sources and that these

Christologies may be arranged in an evolutionary sequence from
"low" to "high". . . . More adequate is an answer which finds,
from the beginning, a Person of such magnitude that, so far from
pious imagination's embroidering and enlarging him, the
perennial problem was, rather, how to teach any insight that
would come near to fathoming him, or any descrption that was
not pitifully inadequate. Successive attempts at word-painting
are (as I read the evidence) not evolving away from the original.
They are all only incomplete representations of the mighty Figure
that has been there all the time.

So, the doctrine of the corporate Christ or the indwelling Christ
— all aspects which are so vital in our experience of Jesus in the
life of the church — are not later "evolutions," but are latent and
implicit at the outset. It is this kind of assessment of a pluralism
of Christologies in the pages of the New Testament which is con-
spicuously lacking in the writings of Cupitt and Wiles, who
always tend to make the bland assumption that early means
primitive, historical and low Christologies, while late means
evolved, ecclesiastical and high Christologies. Moule argues
conclusively that this is a simplistic "myth and that it is imposing
upon the evidence of the New Testament a neatness and a process which is simply not discernible from within the New Testament evidence itself."

However, from quite a different view point and quite differ-
ently-based arguments, Michael Green challenges such a reduced and low Christology as we find in the writings of Cupitt
and Wiles as being no longer even recognizable as Christianity in
any sense in which the church has understood that word. He
writes:

How much can you remove from a car and still possess what is
properly called a car? Lights may be a luxury; you can do without bodywork in warm weather; brakes may be dispensed with,
at all events, on the level; but if you remove the engine or the
chassis it is questionable whether we are still talking about a car
at all.

It is at that level that I would want to criticize the Christology of
Maurice Wiles and Don Cupitt and others in the book *The Myth*

of God Incarnate. I doubt really whether we are left with anything which is recognizable as Christianity at all. I believe that
they have emptied out essential ingredients in the doctrine of the
Incarnation to such a degree that the resulting Christianity and
doctrine which depends upon that Christology is no longer a
Christianity which can use the word meaningfully. I ask myself
whether or not the writers of these essays have recently prepared
anyone for Confirmation or undertaken a preaching or teaching
mission; whether or not they have recently sought to preach
their Christianity in the kind of areas with which my diocese is
most familiar — the docks of the Thames, the deserts of the
inner city or the banal sophistication of middle-class suburbia.

Let me be quite explicit. I am happy to misuse the word *myth*
as Maurice Wiles and his friends have done and to see it as a way
of talking about the truth. No theologian worth his salt would
pretend that doctrines are the truth. That would be to commit
the ultimate idolatry. They are a way of talking about what in
the end of the day we can't talk about at all. The Eastern church,
with its emphasis on "apophatic" theology, is a strong corrective
for a theology which is ever in danger of becoming idolatry. I am
happy to speak, therefore, of the Chalcedonian definition of
Christology as a "myth" open to revision and pointing beyond itself to the one who cannot adequately ever be described or analyzed. Whatever else Jesus is, he is unique and therefore he ex-
plodes all categories before or since. I am happy to do as Maurice Wiles has done; to take the doctrine of transubstantiation
and see it in that sense as a myth — a way of talking about what
in the end I cannot talk about. But, and here we part company, I
do not believe that myths are interchangeable or that all myths
are equally near the truth. Furthermore, I do not believe that it is
impossible to distinguish between myths which keep us from
fundamental error and others which positively encourage error.

I really must, however, deplore the sensational use of the
word *myth* as it was misused in the title of *The Myth of God Incarnate.* Scholars should have a care and concern for language.
In *Webster's Collegiate Dictionary* a myth is defined as "a person
or thing where existence is imaginary or not verifiable." It was
refreshing to see Leslie Houlden's use of the word *pattern* in his

book *Patterns of Faith*. In many ways it is the word *pattern* which would be better in the title of the essays collected together under the general title *The Myth of God Incarnate*, for it is patterns of faith in many ways that the writers are talking about. It is rather a serious charge to accuse scholars of misusing language and not only making it mean what it does not really mean in fact, but also using it in several different and contradictory ways throughout the course of the book. One thing, however, of which I am certain, and even more so since I have spent time in Israel, is that the New Testament narratives are certainly not a myth and that much New Testament criticism (not least Bultman, upon whom Don Cupitt leans somewhat heavily) is totally without foundation. I was fortunate enough to have studied history at Cambridge before I studied theology and I know that the archeological arguments used by New Testament theologians about the dating and strata of the New Testament simply would not stand up in the wider court of appeal of other disciplines, not least history or British literature. It was C. S. Lewis who wrote:

> I have been reading poems, romances, vision literature, legends, myths all my life. I know what they are like. I know that none of them is like this. Of this text there are only two possible views. Either this is reportage — though it may no doubt contain errors — pretty close up to the facts: nearly as close as Boswell. Or else some unknown writer in the 2nd century, without known predecessors or successors, suddenly anticipated the whole technique of modern, novelistic, realistic narrative. If it is untrue it must be narrative of that kind. The reader who does not see this simply has not learnt to read.

I come now to my third concern: the essential ingredients in a Christology which is rooted in the experience of spirituality of the Church and which is capable of proclamation as gospel and good news to the world at large in the name of reconciliation. My most serious indictment of the writings of Maurice Wiles and Don Cupitt is that their myths (dare I call them the myth of Wiles and Cupitt) not only do not replace the Chalcedonian myths with workable formulas that can be communicated from the pulpit in liturgy and song, but they leave us without any of the essential gospel ingredients. In a word there is nothing left to proclaim.

The fundamental ingredients in Chalcedonian Christology are to be found at the level of reconciliation between God and man. This reconciliation is initiated by God because man is helpless to do anything about it. Nevertheless, there are two essential ingredients in such a reconciliation: God and man, between which there has been a wall of separation which, now in Christ, the first fruits of the New Creation, has been broken down — "breaking down the wall of enmity and so making peace." Much contemporary christological reformation simply refuses to hold together the two opposite ends of the paradox and, therefore, fails in the essential ingredient of reconciliation which is at the heart of the experience of the Chalcedonian church. So Dr. John Knox, in his book *Humanity and Divinity of Christ,* would assert: "We can have the humanity without the preexistence and we can have the preexistence without the humanity. There is absolutely no way of having both." On the contrary, however, I would contend that unless we have both we have nothing worth talking about at all. We must admit that the formula we use to enshrine the truth about the person of Christ will at best be clumsy, will most certainly be like nothing else on earth, impossible to comprehend and only just possible to apprehend, precisely because it will be unique. That is the good news — good, because it solves the basic problem, and news, because it has not happened before: 'Behold I am doing some new thing" (Isaiah).

Strangely enough, we are told in the writings of the authors of *The Myth of God Incarnate* that such a formula violates any understanding of the humanity of Jesus. This is rather strange because in fact it is the reverse. I suspect that, if we were in an age with a strong understanding of divinity, we might find it primarily a violation of God and his divinity rather than of man and of his humanity. There is something about truth which always violates our necessarily limited understanding, which is why heresy always fits better and is always more popular. It must be, because it is "made to measure!" "Man cannot bear very much reality" and, whatever christological myth we settle for, we can be certain that the nearer it approximates the truth the more it will violate and split open the "wineskins" of our finite minds. I feel on safer ground when my mind is "blown" and when I feel myself not so much sticking to the facts as finding the facts sticking to me. I feel more at home and on surer ground when I know there is no way by which I can comprehend the formula, but rather that I must seek to apprehend it because, in a strange way, it has already begun to apprehend me. There is something about truth in its fullness which inevitably makes finite man feel that he's been had. One thing you can be certain of is that the 'con' man is always plausible, rational, and has got a sensible story to tell and an explanation for everything. The truth is generally more complex and at some point demands a surrender of a purely cerebral process.

The Incarnation is good news only if there is something in it which violates and changes my view of God. Peter confesses that Christ wanted the myth of contemporary messianic thought to fit neatly and without violence upon the category of the humanity of the person of Jesus in whom he had come to place his trust. Insofar as he permits the largest of his human experiences to reach out and to be clothed with the divine title of Messiah, he is heralded by Jesus as a man of faith with a quality of faith which will make possible the church. But — and here is the rub — insofar as Peter refuses to have the image and idol of Messiah exploded, shattered and reformed so that it could contain suffering and death, he is repudiated by Christ as a temptation of Satan because "he thinks only as men think and not as God thinks." There is the double process of any myth-making in all theology. We cannot do without the myth: but we must at some point abandon it and reach beyond it. The mistake of Peter at Caesaria Philippi is rightly pointed out by Don Cupitt in his essay as the recurring mistake of Christians throughout the ages in refashioning the divinity of Christ in an aloof and untouchable way which would fit comfortably into the mind of a Greek or a Jew. But as Paul realizes, and as gospel experience demands, the God who is united with the man in Jesus is no untouchable God beyond our finite pain but one in whom that pain and sensitivity is already existent at the heart of the universe. P. T. Forsyth writes: "There was a Calvary above which was the mother of it all."

The Church, then, throughout its history has experimented with more easily acceptable doctrines, at one point emphasizing the humanity of Jesus in the sense in which we would define humanity and at another time oscillating to the divinity of Jesus in the way in which we would define divinity. In its better moments the church has realized that both of these categories need to be understood afresh if we are to make sense of the Chalcedonian definition: That is what the news is — a new understanding of God and a new understanding of humanity. It is when I turn to contemporary European attempts to redefine Christology that I find myself on safer ground. I refer of course to Dr. Pannenberg's great work, *Jesus, God and Man,* and also to a remarkable passage from Louis Bouyer's *Le Fils Eternal* (1974) where he shows how our understanding of humanity and of divinity has to be reshaped if we are to grasp the strengths rather than the weaknesses of the Chalcedonian formula. Bouyer writes:

> Many of the difficulties which accumulate from this formula vanish as soon as we recognise that the consciousness of Jesus like every normal consciousness was the consciousness of an object before becoming a consciousness of its own subject. The consciousness of Jesus, as the human consciousness of the Son of God, was before all else consciousness of God. Jesus was the Christ, the Son of the Living God, not directly by knowing that he was but because he knew God as the Father, with everything of the unique and the ineffable that that means for him according to the gospel.

John Macquarrie writes: "He [Jesus] pushes back the horizons of the human mystery so that they open on the divine mystery, but he does this without ceasing to be man" ("thinking about God").

The church, in its experience of reconciliation, its prayer, worship and preaching, knows that in order to do justice to all that experience the good news must both celebrate and proclaim the divinity and the humanity and hold them in a single unity, albeit in tension and with paradox. It does not, however, hold this tension in isolation when it is discussing the person of Jesus and the nature of Christology. There are at least three evidences which converge here and each of them assists the other. There is the person of Jesus ("who do men say that I am?"); there is the nature of the Eucharist ("what is it?"); and there is the character of the Church. All three of these are aspects of the Body of Christ. In all three the truth renders a paradox. In the case of the first we wrestle with the fact that Christ is both man and God. In the case of the second we wrestle with the fact that it is both bread and body. And in the case of the latter we wrestle with our own consciousness that we are both human and divine. What I believe about one I must believe about all three. What I experience of one I experience of all three, for all three are the work of the overshadowing of the Holy Spirit and all three are discerned by faith and not merely by sight. It does not necessarily help me, therefore, to seek a more comfortable formula when I am wrestling about the person of Jesus any more than it helps me to find a more comfortable formula for my experience of the Eucharist or my experience of my own destiny as a member of the Body of Christ. "Now am I the Son of God it does not yet appear what I shall be." In all three cases, for the sake of convenience and tidiness, I can appeal to reductionism so that Jesus becomes merely the best man, the Eucharist becomes merely a special piece of bread and the Church becomes merely an organization of human beings living under the influence and power of the ideology of Jesus of Nazareth. In my heart of hearts, however, I know that this explanation is not large enough to convey what I actually experience. Here was both the embarrassment of Peter at Caesaria Philippi and the embarrassment of the Church in its Chalcedonian definition. I can go to a concert and listen to a violin concerto. When I return to my home and I am asked by a friend what I experienced, I could seek to be logical, scientific and straightforward by replying, "Oh, I merely experienced and simply saw nothing more than one piece of catgut being pulled across another piece of catgut!" On the other hand, I may have to resort to poetry, myth and all kinds of language to convey to my friend the experience which I had enjoyed at the concert.

Yes, strangely enough, the person of Jesus in the experience of the Church has violated both our understanding of God as well as our understanding of humanity. So Michael Ramsey can write:

Is it really credible that one who is God should become man? For myself, as a Christian believer and teacher, I find it to be just credible, as indeed the whole of Christianity is just credible and two reflections help it to be so. The first reflection is that there is antecedently the affinity between God the Creator and man created in his own image after his own likeness. Despite the line between creature and Creator, this affinity is such as to find fulfillment in the closest union between God and man that is conceivable. God is never more characteristically God than when he gives himself to his own and man is revealed in his own potentiality through the union with deity. The second reflection is that if God be self-giving love, the lengths to which he will go in giving himself to his own creation are beyond any of our analogies for what self-giving love will do. The Christian God is not only a God who sends messengers, prophets and teachers to tell the world about himself and his companions; he is a God who comes and gives and takes upon himself the agony of a tormented world of suffering and sin.

In Don Cupitt's writings, especially, I have been struck by how remote and untouchable his picture of God appears to be. Like the Gnostic of old, God seems to be a long way from our grasp or touch. Of course, Cupitt is rightly at pains to chasten theology and remove it from extreme anthropomorphisms; but perhaps in Christian theology (and not least because of the continuity between creation and the Incarnation as being the work of one and the self-same agent) he might do better, as it were, with a "lower" theology of God and a "higher" theology of man. Dare I, with respect, refer him to that oft-quoted phrase, "the glory of God is man come alive"? If we really were created in the image of God then, while still affirming the flaw within that image, it may not be such a long leap from the divine to the human. As David Watson rather strangely puts it: "When God comes down, we go up!" It was Athanasius who was so insistent to write:

> His goodness makes us most fit and things which these wiseacres laugh at as "human" he by his inherent might declares divine. The renewal of creation has been wrought by the selfsame word who made it in the beginning. There is thus no inconsistancy be-

tween creation and salvation; for the one Father has employed the same agent for both works affecting the salvation of the world through the same word who made it at the first."

I realize that Don Cupitt and Maurice Wiles want to retain that essential aspect of incarnational theology which gives value to the material world. And yet here again I have to depart from them. It is true that, in the Old Testament and in much of Judaism, there is the high doctrine of creation. In the Old Testament Theophany helped to endorse the ability of the material world to signify and to convey the world of the Spirit. I would, however, want to emphasize here the other side of the paradox, which I endorsed earlier, by pointing to the scars of the Fall. We want to hold together both the terrifying worth of creation and its terrifying flaws and to assert that nothing less than redemption, reconciliation and renewal from God's initiative by the selfsame Word as with which he created it would enable me to say with confidence at the end of the day, "Gather up the fragments that remain that nothing be lost."

One final word: I do not want to hurl heresies about, but two final strands are vitally important to me in any gospel of the Incarnation. I can only think that the Christology of Maurice Wiles is, in the end, adoptionism in one form or another. The truth about that is that the Church has tried the reduced doctrine of adoptionism many times and found that it has failed; the church has not coped with the evidence or been large enough to carry the weight that redemption demands. It is not good news for me to know that, once upon a time, there lived the best man the world has ever known. I am not good and many people to whom I seek to communicate the gospel are far from good and certainly did not have a good start or a fair start in life. That they are as good as they are is frequently a wonder to me. Neither they nor the world particularly need yet another example. Nothing less than a metaphysical change, in a word, something which changes the whole "chemistry" of man's destiny, is sufficient to convey to broken and flawed mankind that its destiny is still essentially good news. Nothing less, in fact, than a change in the heart of God himself may well say what we are talking about. Any doctrine of the Incarnation which is able to bring about reconciliation must at least be as ambitious in its formula as that and be able to talk of the fundamental and metaphysical change at the heart of the universe in the birth, life, death and resurrection of Jesus Christ. It is true that, at times in history when man seems to be civilized and almost able to pull himself up with his own boot strings, there is a temptation to abandon a high doctrine of the Incarnation. At such moments it almost seems that adoptionism will do and the exemplary view of the atonement goes far enough. However, when I read Golding's *The Lord of the Flies* or newspaper accounts of the events at the People's Temple in Guyana, I realize that man's predicament is far more terrifying than that and that the Incarnation must be a bolder and more profound statement rooted in a metaphysic and not merely a largely cosmetic improvement for the face and image of mankind.

Any Christology which does not enable the trinitarian doctrine of the Godhead to be consequent upon it is, for me, less than Christian. Although, here again, the precise formula is open to change, the experience is foremost and vital. Vladimir Lossky writes: "The Trinity is for the Orthodox church the unshakable foundation of all religious thought, of all piety, of all spiritual life of all experience." Similarly, St. John's sublime record of the words of Jesus: "Father let us have together the love we had before the world began." The good news is that the Trinity has now opened its arm and its heart and, in that wider dimension of the domestic life of the Godhead, reconciliation has finally brought communication and communion for man. That is the experience of prayer, worship and penitence. Putting this another way, Thomas Hancock wrote:

> If there be no absolute co-eternal Son there can be no absolute eternal Father. Unless there be an only begotten Son of God unless this only begotten Son be the one in whom we all consist we may have an unlimited manufacturer — or rather some ommipotent manufacturer may have us as the potter has the vessels but we can have no divine Father.

Yes, unless he is Lord of all, he is not really Lord at all. Let the

Epistle to the Ephesians have the last word. "In saying 'He ascended,' what does it mean but that he had also descended into the lower parts of the earth? He who descended is he who also ascended far above all the heavens, that he might fill all things" (Ephesians 4:9-10).

God Incarnate: Why "Myth"?

Dennis Nineham

Leonard Hodgson, one of my teachers at Oxford, used to say that the characteristic theological judgment is of the form, "This is how I see it; can you not see it that way as well?" That is the spirit in which I hope to speak this morning and my guess is that, when I have finished, a number of you will say, "No, I can't see it that way." If so, that will give rise to a discussion in the course of which I shall certainly expect to learn and I hope that the truth may to some small extent be advanced.

I want to start by offering you an example or parable. Suppose that one of you were suddenly to feel ill, thrash about for a while and then lose consciousness and fall off your chair onto the ground. What should we do or say? I suppose we should clear a space around you, loosen anything tight around your neck and dampen your forehead in the hope that you had merely fainted and would soon come round. If you did not, we should send for a doctor and the doctor would examine you, talk to your friends, maybe call up your own doctor and eventually diagnose, let us say, a diabetic coma. If so, an appropriate amount of sugar or insulin would be injected and, probably within twenty minutes or half an hour, you would, be sitting up and taking notice, not really much the worse for what had happened.

Now I want to ask you to think what would have happened if exactly the same situation had occurred, let us say, in England in the sixteenth or seventeenth century; if someone then had been in exactly the same medical condition, what would people have said and done? I suppose, at first, they would have done the same as in our first example; but then, if the person in question had not regained consciousness, they would have said, "Ah poor fellow, the balance of his humors is disturbed," and they would have sent for what they called a "chirurgeon," who would have come with a formidable object known as a cupping-glass, or perhaps with some leeches, and drawn off a great deal of blood. What good would that have done? Not much, I imagine, if the case was one of diabetes; nevertheless that is the way they would have understood and responded to the situation.

Suppose now that exactly the same thing had happened in first-century Palestine. What would people have said and done then? At first, much the same as we should. Then, if consciousness did not return, they would have said, "Ah poor fellow, he's possessed of a demon," and they would have fallen to prayer over the patient and, if that did no good, they would no doubt have said, "This is a very powerful demon, or maybe it's even a legion of demons," and they would have sent for some well-known exorcist who would have come and performed the appropriate rituals and recited the right prayers. Again, who knows what the results would have been; but if it was a case of diabetes, I'm not very optimistic.

By the year 2500 let us hope that diabetes will be a thing of the past. If it's not, and diabetic comas are still occurring, I have no idea of what people will say and do then; but you may be quite sure that it will be different from what we do, or people in the past have ever done.

You see the point of all this? Exactly the same thing is involved — a person in exactly the same medical condition. The condition is an important and serious one and yet, in different periods and different cultures, people understand it, respond to it and treat it in widely different ways.

I want to ask you to think about that example rather carefully. Don't brush it aside as just a scientific or medical thing, with no significance for deeper or more spiritual issues. Rather, ask yourself *why* the people in the different periods I have mentioned would have responded to this thing in different ways. If you do, you will soon come to the conclusion that they would have responded differently to this because they responded differently to everything. Their outlook on this would be different because they would have different views about chemistry, physics, psychology, ethics, astronomy, demonology — virtually anything you could mention. The fact is that you cannot understand one thing in a given civilization in a way that does not make sense in the light of the way you understand other things. It would, for example be simply impossible to hold a four-humors view of disease in the context of modern scientific medicine.

What is involved here is a fairly recent realization, namely that every period, every culture, has a basic perspective which controls the way that it understands practically everything in existence. And in each culture that basic perspective is controlled by what philosophers call the "absolute presuppositions" of that culture. Let me quote the philosopher T. E. Hulme:

> There are certain doctrines which for a particular period seem not doctrines, but inevitable categories of the human mind. Men do not look on them merely as correct opinion, for they have become so much part of the mind and lie so far back that they are never really conscious of them at all. They do not see them, but other things *through* them. It is these abstract ideas at the centre, the things which they take for granted, that characterise a period. There are in each period certain doctrines, a denial of which is looked on by the men of that period just as we might look on the assertion that two and two make five. It is these abstract things at the centre, these *doctrines* felt as *facts,* which are the source of all the other. . . characteristics of a period.[1]

It follows, you see, that if the "Doctrines felt as facts" — the absolute presuppositions — change, the perspective is changed and so is the way in which everything is understood. In fact, you might define a civilization as a way of understanding things — or rather an interrelated set of understandings — under the control of a particular set of primary, or absolute, presuppositions; and let me remind you that "absolute presuppositions" lie so deep that we can scarcely at all be aware of what our absolute presuppositions are.

---

[1]*Speculations: Essays on Humanism and the Philosophy of Art* (Boston: Routledge & Kegan, 1936), pp. 50-51.

The relevance of all this for our subject will, I hope, be obvious as soon as we substitute for the diabetic coma of my parable the life, activity and death of Jesus of Nazareth. And it will become clear how, in my opinion, Christology should be defined: It is the study of the way that Jesus' life and activity have been understood against various cultural backgrounds at various times, and the study of the way they should be understood against the contemporary cultural background. (Of course when I use the last phrase I am thinking of the cultural background of advanced Western civilization; no doubt other understandings are appropriate in what we call less developed civilizations in other parts of the contemporary world.)

To start at the beginning, we have one understanding of Jesus of Nazareth in the New Testament — or rather we have a set of understandings of him which are fairly closely related because they are all more or less controlled by the same, or roughly similar, absolute presuppositions. To read the New Testament is to realize at once that the basic response of Jesus' followers to what he had done and been was a feeling of joy, gratitude and release. The early Christians felt release from bondage to demonic forces, from the burden of sin and guilt, from fear of the future and especially fear of death, and from the need for any attempt to justify themselves and earn God's good will. As far as God was concerned, they had a sense of being in the closest communion with him; they knew him as a father who could be relied upon to give his children all the blessings of salvation just because they were his children and he was a generous father — whatever their sins or shortcomings might have been. As for the future, they could face it without fear, even though most of them thought that the end of the world, and with it the terrible judgment of God, would come in their own lifetime. In the light of what Jesus had been and said and done, they were clear that, when that moment came, they would be accounted righteous and admitted to the Kingdom to share in its blessings. As for their attitude toward other people, since they were freed from all need to secure, insure and justify themselves, which means in fact to exploit other people, they were free really to treat their neighbors as other people, that is, people as important and real as themselves, with real needs, and they were free to tend to those needs and generally to reproduce in their relations with others the same love and generosity that they were conscious of receiving at the hand of God. In fact, they felt themselves to have been reborn, to be new creatures.

But these were men of a particular culture. Perhaps I could call it a metaphysical culture or, better, a mythological culture. As such, they believed not just that all blessings come from God, but that they could penetrate, as it were, behind the supernatural scenes and discover and reveal the process by which God made his blessings available. You get the same sort of thing in the Old Testament. For example, the Jews were not merely conscious, as many people have been, that the whole of creation depended on the creative activity of God; they believed that they could get behind the supernatural scenes and discover just how and when God had initiated the creative process. In the same way, as Wheeler Robinson taught us, it was one of the claims of the Hebrew prophets that they somehow had access behind the scenes to the heavenly *sodh,* the council at which Yahweh, the God of Israel, and his heavenly advisors discussed and decided their plans for men; and it was because the prophets could be there behind the scenes that they could lay bare to their fellows what went on at the council.

As with the Old Testament writers and the first creation, so with the New Testament writers and the new creation. Just as the Old Testament writers, in relating their picture, relied on various traditions which they found in existence, modified in the light of their experience of Yahweh their God, so the New Testament writers, in their attempt to explain the workings by which the new creation had been produced, relied on traditions which they found available in their cultural milieu, modified in the light of their experience of Jesus of Nazareth. As you well know, many Jewish sects in the century or two before Christ had been expecting that God would very soon intervene decisively to put everything right. Many of them thought he would do it in person; but others thought that he would do it through some agent or representative who would appear in the world, gather round him the righteous remnant and initiate the end of history and the coming of the new era in which everything would be completely in conformity with God's will — which was therefore referred to as the rule, or Kingdom, of God. Then, it was thought, God's representative and the righteous remnant would enter the Kingdom to share the blessings of the new era with Yahweh himself. It is vital to recognize that it was against that background, and in their specific culture, that the New Testament writers and other early Christians interpreted Jesus. You remember the question attributed to John the Baptist in the Gospels: "Art thou he that should come or look we for another?" The early Christians replied emphatically, yes, Jesus *was* the one who was to come, the representative so many people in the world of first-century Judaism had been expecting God to send.

It is important not to oversimplify the picture, however. Among first-century Jews there was a great variety of images of God's expected intervention. Some thought that he would send down into the world a preexistent figure who had been with him from the creation. Others thought that he would raise up in the world some king or prophet or priest, much as he had raised up Moses or David or one of the older prophets. And just as the Jews varied in their images, so they varied in the nomenclature they used. Some spoke of the Son of David, some of a Son of God, others of a Son of Man, others of the Messiah or Christ, and so forth. As we would expect, this variety of names and images reflected in the New Testament interpretation of Jesus. Some New Testament writers, Paul for example, or Mark, see him as some sort of preexistent figure, the Son of God sent into the world, though Paul never makes very clear (even if Philippians is accepted as Pauline) exactly what the relation between this Son of God and Yahweh was in the days before Jesus' early life. Other writers, Matthew and Luke for example, see the matter quite differently. They seem not to think that Jesus had preexisted at all. They think his life began with his conception in the womb of his mother. For them he is the Son of God, a supernatural being, surely enough, but in the sense that, in his case, God or his spirit took the part normally taken by a human male in the conception of a child. Jesus was, if I may put it so without offense, divine on his father's side, though that is not the only —

or even perhaps the most important — thing Matthew's and Luke's birth naratives were intended to convey. And then, as we all know, the Gospels of Matthew and Luke contain material which seems to come from other early Christians who thought of Jesus as a supernatural figure — Son of God or Son of Man — but in such a way that his birth had been perfectly normal, with a human mother *and* a human father. At the other end of the spectrum in the New Testament you get John and the writer to the Hebrews, both of whom clearly think that Jesus was a pre-existent being sent into the world by God to redeem it; and in John you even begin to get, though in a very tentative and impre-cise form, some discussion of what the relation between the pre-existent Son of God and his Father had been before Jesus became flesh.

The New Testament writers all agree, more or less, about the course of events once Jesus had appeared on the scene. He deployed miraculous powers against the demonic forces; he taught with unique authority, as would be expected of God's representative; and, finally, when men brought about his death, he accepted it willingly and freely as sacrifice and expiation for the sins of the world. Then three days or, some say, four days after his death, he was raised from the dead to God's right hand on high. Some of the New Testament writers say this happened directly, all in one fell swoop, so to speak; some seem to envis-age an interlude of about thirty-six hours, others envisage an interlude of forty days. Their portrayals vary, but they all agree that, once seated at the right hand of God, Jesus was not inac-tive. From heaven he was working for his people, strengthening them, guiding them, helping them; they could appeal to him as their Lord in the same sort of way that people of other religions appealed to the many lords and gods of their faiths. In par-ticular, Jesus, now seated at God's right hand, had become a sort of new corporate personality, a vine into which through faith and baptism Christians could be incorporated so that they could share in his perfection and his perfect relationship with his Father, instead of sharing in the sin and guilt of the first Adam as they had done before.

About one thing we must be clear, and that is that none of

these writers supposed that Jesus was God *tout court,* Yahweh in person come to earth; any such notion would have been quite unthinkable for anyone in the New Testament period. What is more, we must recognize that, as the very variety of these views shows, they are interpretations, inspired interpretations if you like, but nevertheless human interpretations or understandings of who or what Jesus had been and the meaning of what he had done. If you stop to think about it, what else could they be? You can't actually *see* the preexistent Son of God becoming flesh; nor, despite Luke's rather naive picture, can you *see* Jesus ascending to God's right hand. You can't *see* the ascended Lord being, or becoming, a new corporate personality. These are bound to be images, pictures, interpretations which were put upon the figure of Jesus of Nazareth by some of his earliest followers.

I think we must frankly admit that they are not interpretations which we can now accept. The reason for that is basically that the absolute presuppositions on which these interpretations were based are different from those which we hold in our culture. First-century Jews and Christians believed in the most realistic way that God was about to send an agent, or representative, into the world to end history and to bring in the new era; and that belief, in the form in which they held it, is something that we can no longer share. Professor John Knox puts the point very well in a passage in which he is describing how one of his colleagues had been talking along lines similar to my above arguments and someone in the audience asked: "But then, supposing that Jesus really was the Son of Man?" John Knox writes:

> I find such a question very hard to deal with, not because of what it asks for, but because of what it seems to pre-suppose. It seems to ascribe to the "Son of Man" objective and personal reality. It seems to assume that there was, and is, a Son of Man, but what does the phrase "Son of Man" . . . really designate? Must we not say that it stands for an idea, or an image, in the minds of certain ancient Jews? One can trace to some extent the beginnings and development of this idea or image in Jewish culture, but do we

for a moment suppose that it is the name of any actual person, that the Son of Man in fact exists or ever existed?[2]

That just about hits the nail on the head but, in the light of what I was saying earlier, I hope you will agree that there is nothing daunting about it. Even if the terms in which the New Testament Christians understood and interpreted the figure and work of Jesus are no longer possible for us, that does not mean that they were not pointing to, and seeking to interpret, something of the utmost reality and the utmost significance. As we have seen, we can no longer regard a diabetic coma as a case of a "disturbance of the humors," but that does not mean that, when people talked about a disturbance of the humors, they were not talking about something which was very real, very significant and very serious. In the light of my parable of the diabetic coma, I suppose that what we have to do at this point is to ask the question that Leonard Hodgson used to tell us to ask: "What must the truth be now if people who thought as they did put it like that?" I commend that form of words to you, even if it has now become a bit hackneyed, and even if, as some scholars think, it might be more precisely phrased. At least as it stands it has the merit of being memorable.

Before we can begin to deal with it, however, there is a great deal more to be said, and I rather quail at the thought of trying to put it into a short space. The realization that different periods and cultures understand things in different lights is a modern one; it scarcely goes back beyond Giovanni Battista Vice in the eighteenth century. In the first century, and many centuries after that, people were unaware of it; they supposed that, once an understanding and interpretation of something had been arrived at, that could be the right understanding and interpretation of it for all time and in all circumstances. And so the Christians of the New Testament period accepted the New Testament account of Jesus as giving simply *the* truth about him. It's a very easy trap to fall into even now: When we talk about a diabetic coma, we easily think that is just what it is in absolute terms. We forget that in

---

[2]*The Death of Christ: The Cross in New Testament History and Faith* New York: Abington, 1958), pp. 71-72.

five hundred years' time people will think of it quite differently, just as people thought of it differently five hundred years ago. We simply think of our understanding of it as *the* truth about it, and that is the way the New Testament Christians thought about Jesus when they called him Son of God, Son of Man, Son of David and so on. What is more, this process was reinforced as the years went by and the New Testament came in effect to be canonized, and the descriptions and understandings of Jesus in the New Testament were thought to be guaranteed by God himself. All that remained to be done, according to the early theologians, was to understand the New Testament interpretations and titles of Jesus as fully as possible, to draw out their meaning, to dot the *i*s and cross the *t*s in order to clarify anything that had so far been ambiguous or only implicit.

From the perspective of our culture, however, their understanding of what they were doing is not adequate. Have you ever thought of what would have happened if, instead of going west soon after the lifetime of Jesus, Christianity had gone east, for example to India, where Buddha was just in the process of being deified, or perhaps south to Arabia? In either case, it would have met cultures with very different absolute presuppositions from those of the West, and how different a thing Christian theology would have been! What in fact happened in the early Christian centuries, however, was that the Christian movement, with its increasingly canonized New Testament, moved west into a culture different from that in which it arose, into a Greek culture, where on the whole (and I speak at this point very much subject to Dr. Norris' correction) the people who led Christian thought and interpreted the person of Jesus came from a Greek, and particularly a Platonic, background. That is admittedly something very broad to say, because there were various kinds of Platonism and, in any case, Platonism was mixed with many other streams of thought. Nevertheless, I will risk a generalization. These thinkers often used, as a model for reality, the sun in the sky and the warmth and light and energy that flow down from it to keep us in this world alive and active. According to their belief, although life, power and warmth were thus emanating from the sun all the time, the sun remained totally undiminished and unchanged in the process. What is more, they noticed that, if you try to look at the sun, look straight into it, you can't see the sun because it is too bright; you are simply blinded. In the same way, they believed, there was an ultimate source of being from which all life, all existence and all energy emanated, but in such a way that that source was not changed or diminished or influenced in any way whatsoever; moreover, this source of all being was so transcendent that men could never see it — it could never come within their ken. So far as men could have contact with the divine, it was always in the form of lesser, secondary, divine beings, of whom there were various numbers with various names in different systems, but in many systems there were two.

Perhaps I could try to put some of this in diagramatic form.

In this world there is a divide between the "really real" supernatural realm and the natural realm of "coming to be and passing away." This divide was sometimes placed between B and C. (c.f., for example, the uncertainty of the Christian Father Origen about the full divinity of the Holy Spirit.)

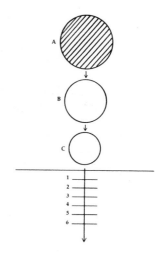

At the top you have the supreme being, the source of all other existents, totally undiminished, unchanged and unchangeable, yet with the other existents streaming from it. This being in turn gives rise to a lesser divine being, and that gives rise to a still lesser divine being; and then, below the line as it were, you get the created world, the world of relative unreality, in which there are creatures at various levels as you go down the hierarchy, or chain, of being — higher divine beings, lower divine beings, then lower still, first angels then other supernatural beings, then human beings, animal beings, vegetable beings, and so on.

We naturally ask what distinguished the beings at these various levels from one another. Very briefly, and at the risk of gross oversimplification, the idea was that the beings on each level were constituted of a different *ousia,* or substance. If you take a cube of wood and throw it into water, because it is made of wood it will float; if you take a cube of iron and throw that into water, because it is made of a different substance, iron, it will sink. In the same way, the qualities and abilities of any being in the hierarchy depended on the *ousia* of which it was constituted. If you were constituted of human substance, then you had power to reason, to understand and to think; you had freedom, free will, freedom to move. On the other hand, you were liable to be influenced, to be tempted, to be led into sin, and you were subject to decay and, ultimately, death. If you were constituted of the substance stone, then although your shape might be that of a man (if you were a statue) you had no power to think or understand or move or be free; although you would decay in time, the time would be a very much longer one, as we know from the survival of ancient statues.

What I want to emphasize is that this general picture — and I cannot overemphasize the word *general* — was for those thinkers simply an account of the way things were. They took this picture as being part of the given, in the way in which we take the law of gravity, for example, as simply part of the given. We don't think of it as an interpretation, but just as the way things are; and that is how they regarded their view of things. The upshot was that any religion which was to be believed by people with this sort of background had to be capable of being related to this sort of "map" of reality. It had to be capable of being stated in terms of this way of viewing things. And I think it's not unfair to say that, in the first five, six or seven centuries, Christian theology consisted essentially of translating the contents of the New Testament and of the Christian tradition into the terms of this map. To some extent the process of translation seemed obvious enough. The being at the top (A) must be God the Father; in the early days it seemed obvious that the second being (B) must be God the Son, the third being (C) the Spirit, and so on with the angels and archangels, the lesser supernatural beings, human beings and so forth (1, 2, 3, 4, 5, 6 . . .). One had to translate a tradition which emerged in a Jewish culture into terms belonging to this different sort of background.

If Jesus as Son of God was identified with this lesser though still divine being, what about the fact that he was also the Son of Man, that he was human? The problem presented itself that Jesus was, or possessed, two beings: He was constituted of two substances because in him the secondary divine being (B) had come down and united himself with human substance. And for these thinkers it was absolutely essential that it should have been so. For, as they understood it, if human substance, human beings, are to be saved, that can only be because they have come to share in divine substance, because they have come to be freed from their ability to be influenced and tempted, they have come to be freed from decay, death, change and so on. They must take on the perfections and unchangeability of the divine existence.

An analogy these thinkers frequently used to illustrate the point was that of iron in a fire. If you take a piece of iron in its ordinary state, it's hard, cold, grey-colored and so on. If you want it to take on the qualities of fire, if you want it to become white or red and soft and hot and glowing, then you have to plunge the iron into the fire. The iron and the fire have to come together in a union. And that, in their view, was what had had to happen in the case of Jesus Christ. Human substance and divine substance had to be brought together into a union so that, just as the iron took on the qualities of the fire, the humanity could take on the qualities of the divinity.

As you know, however, the Fathers more and more came to

realize that it would not do to think of the Son of God as a sec
ondary divine being. How could there be degrees of divineness?
With what could divinity be diluted? In any case, if a lesser di
vine being had been united with our humanity, it would not have
been the real Godhead with which we were united. If Jesus was
not really God himself, then he could not give real divinity to
man. That is how the Fathers reasoned; and accordingly, more
and more they came to feel that the picture had to be changed
They had to think not of lesser divine beings, but of God himsel
in three *hypostases,* three centers of being — Father, Son and
Holy Spirit — and it was the second of these who, in person, had
come down and joined himself with human substance in what
came to be called the Incarnation.

There is not enough space to discuss the rights and wrongs of
all this, but one thing I do want to make clear is that I do not for
a moment suggest that the theology of these thinkers was simply
a matter of abstract speculation. In fact, deep religious values
were involved. These thinkers were concerned to preserve the
truth that it was genuinely God, the one true God, with whom
they met, and were reconciled, in Christ. They were so sure that
God cared that, although in their basic thinking he was unchangeable, and as such incapable of initiative, they dared to say
that he had come down and had, in some measure, partaken in
the lot and the suffering of his human creatures. In trying to hold
together these various considerations, they got themselves involved in all sorts of difficulties and inconsistencies and indeed, I
think, logical impossibilities, though that is obviously a controversial opinion. What I want to make clear is that this whole
way of thinking about things, and indeed the doctrine of the Incarnation itself in its classical form as we find it in the creeds, is
part and parcel of one particular cultural outlook — not that of
the New Testament, not that of our time, but that of Greek
thinkers brought up on the Greek philosophy of the early Christian centuries. The doctrine of the Incarnation in its classical
form is essentially relative to that particular cultural background.

In connection with this point, it should be noted that, as soon
as the Christian Fathers, the producers of the creeds, had done

their work, the Roman Empire fell and was succeeded by what are called the Dark Ages and the Middle Ages. No doubt these were not as dark as they have sometimes been painted, but nevertheless there was little question at this time of there being much cultural progress or development in Europe. The peoples of Europe had all they could do to hold on to the wisdom and the insights of the ancients, to preserve them in writing and in memory and to understand and expound upon them as best they could. The period that followed that of the Fathers was one intensely convinced of its inferiority to what had gone before; men felt that the great ones of the past — Aristotle and Plato in philosophy, Hippocrates and Galen in medicine, Jesus, Paul, Athanasius and Augustine in theology — had been wiser than anyone alive at that time and that what they said was not to be questioned. And so in this period of at least a thousand years — and, I would argue, even more — the general picture I have been describing, and the way of interpreting the New Testament (very strange in our eyes) on which it was based, were accepted as being the core and center of Christianity. People read the New Testament through the eyes of the Christian Fathers and, incidentally, had to do some pretty astonishing things with it (by our standards) in order to get this picture out of it. But they accepted that as being the only way, the right way, to understand the New Testament, and they accepted the picture which emerged as constituting what Christianity essentially is. And that goes not only for the Orthodox Churches of the East and for the Roman Catholic Church, but for the Reformed Churches as well. Much as Luther and Calvin might object to many of the beliefs of the medieval theologians and the Fathers, they were sufficiently part of the cultural scene I have been sketching to believe that the New Testament meant what the Creed and the Fathers said it meant and that the picture which emerged from their writings was the true picture, the picture which could be traced back to the New Testament and eventually to Jesus himself. Thus, for nearly twelve hundred years there was in the Christian consciousness a sense that the essence of Christianity, *the articulus stantis aut cadentis ecclesiae,* was the belief that the second person of the Trinity, God the Son, united himself with our substance and became flesh and dwelt among us.

If a community believes something for twelve hundred years,
that thing goes pretty deep into its consciousness; to this day
many Christians still believe, as was believed in that period, that
the Incarnation is the core of Christianity and that believing in it
is an essential part of what it means to be a Christian. For example, in my own country Robert Morgan, one of our ablest
younger theologians, has just produced a series of papers in
which he argues that, although you can no longer accept all the
details of the creeds of the period of the Fathers, it is nevertheless
the essence of Christianity that, in the most profound sense, a
metaphysical objective sense, Jesus was God and man, united in
this person.

I must be frank and say that I find this a very strange position,
if only because it unchurches first of all the New Testament writers themselves, who certainly never believed any such thing, and
also many of the people who lived in the centuries immediately
after the New Testament. It also unchurches many profoundly
pious Christians of the last two and a half centuries or so, because — and here I come to the third part of what I want to say
— by about the year 1750 the ax was laid to the root of the tree.

At that time a new cultural movement, a profoundly new cultural movement, which had started at least as far back as the
thirteenth century and which had broken surface in quite a big
way at the time of the so-called Renaissance, finally burst into
full vigor and began to accelerate change at an astonishing rate.
As you know, the rate of acceleration has progressively in-
creased and so there have been produced the bewilderingly rapid
cultural changes of our technological age. I wish I had both the
time and the competence to talk further about this process of
change, if only to convince you that the rate and scale of change
is likely to be, if anything, greater in the coming century than it
has been in the past. You will find some very illuminating remarks about it in an essay by C. S. Lewis, the first essay in his
book *They Asked for a Paper,* where it is documented and set
out in a very lively fashion. Although I do not by any means
agree with Lewis's proposals for dealing with the matter, I am
sure he is right in saying that this is the most important single

phenomenon with which modern Christian theology has to deal. We live in a new age of cultural development and in a very real sense this means that all things have become new and we are faced with new problems.

The movement, I suppose, had three main prongs. First, the scientific which does not perhaps immediately concern us, except insofar as natural science has shown by its experimental work that the ancients, far from always being right, had almost always been wrong where scientific matters were concerned. As soon as you tested Aristotle, for example, by experiment you found just how wrong he was. And that meant that, under the influence of people like Nicholas of Cusa, Francis Bacon and the members of the Royal Society in England, the great sense of the authority of the past, the sense that the "people back there" were the people who knew, very quickly began to break down; our society has become a present- and a future-oriented, rather than a past-oriented, society. That is something that the Christian Church has not even begun to face up to yet.

Second, as regards philsophy and psychology and in general the study of those elements in this world which are not amenable to investigation by the natural sciences, there has been much less agreement than in the area covered by natural science; but there have been changes and many advantages and, in particular, a sense on the part of most thinkers that we can no longer hold on to the substance of philosophy of the past and the picture of reality underlying traditional Christian doctrine. Certainly it was quickly realized, as the modern world developed, that we cannot hold on to the notion of a grading or hierarchy of being. We can no longer think in terms of such concepts. Even if we want to think in terms of substance, the *onus probandi* will be firmly on our shoulders and we shall have to put up a very good case for it in the face of a philosophical establishment which is firmly opposed to it.

The third and last prong is a relatively modern one, namely the historical, which does not originate much earlier than the nineteenth century. The problem here arose when historians began to follow the scientists in refusing to rest on authority. They felt bound to make clear that they could not accept accounts of the past simply because they were on hand, however ancient or sacred or hoary they may have been; they felt obliged always to test evidence about the past. The modern historian is rather like a law court: A law court does not simply take the evidence of one witness and say "that is the truth." It takes the evidence of this witness and that witness and the other witness; it looks at the motor car after the crash, or whatever it may be, and it puts all the evidence together; it compares it, contrasts it, it "tortures" it as R. G. Collingwood used to say; and, in the light of that, it forms its own view of what happened, a view which is almost never exactly the same as that of any single witness. This is the way historians now proceed. As soon as the critical study of history emerged, historians began to say: Give us all the written accounts of the past and all the archeological and other unwritten evidence; we will then test, sift and torture this material and, only after that, shall we be able to come up with our own account. Today we have to accept — we simply *have* to accept — that on this basis the modern historian can often tell us what happened in the past much more accurately than the people who lived at the time or the people who came immediately afterward. Especially in the light of his understanding of such phenomena as soil erosion, the effects of deforestation on climate or the effects of economic inflation, the historian can often understand what was happening in a past era in a way that people who lived at that time could not understand it themselves. Such a claim is not arrogant; it is simply the truth and we have no alternative but to come to terms with it. And, of course, it applies to the Bible and the history of the Christian doctrine as well as to everything else.

Consequently, the representatives of the new cultural movement, as it broke surface, found themselves unable to accept the Christian tradition, as it stood for three reasons.

1. *Philosophical:* They found themselves unable to accept the philosophical categories in terms of which it was expressed.

2. *Historical:* They found themselves unable to accept the attitude to historical sources on which it was based — for example, that every word of the New Testament was historically accurate and guaranteed by God — and also, in many cases, the

historical conclusions to which such an attitude to the sources had given rise.

3. *Exegetical:* They found themselves unable to accept the interpretative principles on the basis of which tradition Christology had been extracted from the Scriptures.

What then was to be done? In a period as impressed, one might almost say obsessed, by the methods of historical study as the nineteenth century was, the answer seemed fairly obvious. Historical techniques had to be applied to the New Testament and other available evidence in order to rediscover Jesus as he really was — the Jesus of history, as he came to be called. It seemed at the time that, once he had been discovered or reconstructed, it would be obvious what claims, natural or supernatural it was necessary or plausible to make on his behalf. With this in mind, literally hundreds of writers attempted to penetrate the historical Jesus in the hope of being able to find out for themselves what sort of interpretation or claims he called for in the culture of the nineteenth century. Here again, I wish I could discuss the matter in more detail, but I dare say you know your Schweitzer as well as I do. In the upshot, the goal proved impossible to attain. The New Testament documents are not the sort that enable you to reconstruct the historical Jesus with the accuracy or detailed precision envisaged. We all, no doubt, have our notions of what the Jesus of history was like; I certainly have. But the point is that, if we were to take a poll, we should find that no two people in this room would agree on the matter, and the range of disagreement would be even greater if we were to go outside Christian circles. The fact is that the New Testament document were written for religious reasons, to make religious points, and, what is more, they cover only a very very small part of Jesus' life. B. H. Streeter once calculated that everything said and done in the Gospels, apart from the period of forty days in the wilderness, about which we have in any case no details, could be fitted into a period of about three weeks, which means that the overwhelmingly greater part of Jesus' life is totally hidden from us. On the basis of that sort of evidence, and in the absence of all official records, newspaper files and means of cross-checking which a modern historian requires, there proved to be no way of providing the basis for a reconstruction of the Jesus of history such as would make unmistakably clear what theological claims it is appropriate to make for him. That again of course is a controversial judgment, but I suppose there is hardly a New Testament scholar alive who would not agree with it in greater or lesser degree.

And so, although brevity will compel me to do it in too sharp a form, I want to pose to you this question: If we cannot with integrity accept the traditional Christ of the creeds and the Fathers, and if we cannot recover the Jesus of history so as to see what he was like and be able to interpret him for ourselves, what are we to do? You will not be able to understand a great deal of modern Lutheran theology, whether Barthian or Bultmannian, unless you realize that those are the questions from which it starts. I shall not take time here to discuss the various conclusions to which it comes because I believe that, illuminating as many of them are, they are in the last resort mistaken.

I shall conclude by saying that, as I see it, we have to take the situation in which we find ourselves as part of the guidance of God. There is no need for us to be bothered or despairing; we can be relaxed. Our situation is one to which God in his providence has brought us and our concern must simply be to deal with it in a way which corresponds to his will.

At one point, at any rate, our feet are on bedrock. If you interpret the event of Jesus as including not just his own words and deeds and death in isolation — which would in any case be a false historical abstraction — but include in it the impact that he made on his contemporaries, their understanding of him and all the results which issued from his life, then you can say with absolute assurance that from these things there arose a community in which, as we have seen, a new relationship with God, the world and neighbor were known and treasured. That is just plain historical fact. It is also true that that community, and the relationship with God known within that community, have continued to our day and that we share in that relationship to God. The relationship with God in the Christian church has approved itself to countless people of different cultures and all the ages and so it has survived — still a distinctively *Christian* relationship with God.

In each culture, however, in each age through which Christianity has passed, men have had to rethink, reunderstand and restate both their relationship with God and indeed the God to whom they were relating. They have tended to do it for the most part unconsciously, but in our age we cannot help being self-conscious about it. I tried to show how something of this sort took place in the age of the Fathers, who lived in a culture very different from that of the New Testament and who therefore vitally transformed Christianity, though without altogether realizing what they were doing. The same thing happened during the Reformation; the same thing happened during the Enlightenment; in a small way, the same thing happened in the nineteenth century, when our grandfathers and great-grandfathers had to reexamine their understanding of God, rethink and restate it so as to take account of new insights into the immense antiquity and infinite size of the universe. The way it had come to be as it is now was the result of evolution and the process of natural selection. If Christians in each period had not been prepared to make the necessary changes, whether consciously or not, Christianity could not have survived and the Christian relationship with God could not have been passed down to you and me in a form which made it a live option for us, something that we could with integrity accept and treasure and which, I take it, has become to all of us the deepest and most important thing in our lives.

The suggestion — perhaps you will think a revolutionary suggestion — I want to make in conclusion is that our priority as Christians, and as Christian theologians in contemporary Western culture, should be the understanding of our relationship with God in a way which makes sense in our world. It should be the attempt to practice our relationship with God in a way that is compatible with the rest of our approach to life. Ours is an age which is acutely, and I think rather healthily, aware of the strict limitation of its ability to probe behind the supernatural scenes and see the inner workings by which God produces his results. In the ancient world they thought they could do it. In the modern world, especially if we've read our Wittgenstein, we know, or at any rate we strongly suspect, that we can't, and I believe that is something to be taken seriously. Such abilities as we do possess to probe the things of God, to understand the supernatural world and its workings, should be employed in order to answer the religious question our contemporaries really care about: "What does it mean to talk of God? Not of Christ but of God — in a world which is, so to speak, infinite both in space and time, in which all scientific events are interrelated in what seems to be an unbroken web, and in which all historical events are interrelated in what seems to us to be an unbroken web of motivation and causation?"[3] In *this* world, the world of *our* culture, what does it mean to speak of God, and in particular what does it mean to talk of God acting in and toward this world, intervening in it? In the modern world, as David Friedrich Strauss put it, in a typically caustic phrase, *die Wohnungsnot ist fur Gott eingetreten* ("the housing problem has arisen for God"): Where is he in this infinite world? How do we speak of God in relation to this world? It seems to me that theologians who are wrestling with this sort of question — people in this country like Gordon Kaufman at Harvard, Langdon Gilkey at University of Chicago, Schubert Ogden at Southern Methodist University; people in my own country like John Hick, Maurice Wiles, Don Cupitt, John Macquarrie — are the people who are putting their theological shoulders to the right wheel. This is where our energies need to be directed. How are we to knit up the relationship to God which we have inherited, treasured and tried to deepen in the Christian tradition, with the insights which we also inevitably have as members of advanced Western technological society?

To my mind the question *how* our relationship to God came to be the way it is, *how* through Jesus of Nazareth God produced this relationship with himself in the church, is a question which scarcely deserves the high priority and the enormous amount of attention that it seems to be receiving in a great deal of contemporary theology. Of course historians will wish to continue their efforts to discover all they possibly can about the man

---

[3] The reference is not to predestination, but to the fact that every contemporary historian assumes without question that all historical events have their motives and causes which interrelate them with all other historical events.

Jesus of Nazareth. Quite recently, for example, two Roman Catholic scholars have done interesting work on this question: Father Lucas Grollenberg in Holland and, right here in San Francisco, Professor J. P. Mackey, with his very interesting book *Jesus, the Man and the Myth*. If I understand them right, both these scholars believe that it is possible to account for the way the Christian relationship with God arose from Jesus, wholly, or almost wholly, through the normal processes of history and the way God habitually works through them by way of providence, without assuming any of the special categories or statuses that traditional theology has ascribed to Jesus, from New Testament times onwards. It strikes me as interesting that two Roman Catholic theologians, working so far apart, should simultaneously come to that conclusion. But, for me, suffice it to say that Jesus must have been all that he needed to be in the providence of God in order to give rise to the church and to the new relationship with God that has originated from him in the church. The church, as I have tried to show, has ever and again rethought and reformulated that relationship, and it is our duty to reformulate and rethink it in terms appropriate to our culture. In this context I am perfectly content simply to re-echo the words of Professor John Knox when he was at Union Theological Seminary: "The divinity of Jesus was the purpose and activity of God which made the event which happened round him, but also in and through him, the saving event it was." And then at greater length:

> That this event had the particular result it had — a new community in which are found a new forgiveness, victory and hope — is a matter of empirial knowledge in the Church; but why this particular event had this particular result is a matter altogether beyond our knowing. God's thoughts are not our thoughts and his ways are not our ways. The event was a whole event and its effect was a whole effect. We cannot break the event into parts and attribute the whole effect to one part, nor can we ascribe any particular part of the effect to any particular part of the event. Both event and effect are one and indivisible; and moreover, they belong indissolubly together. Of this whole the remembered death of Jesus is the poignant center.[4]

---

[4]*The Death of Christ*, pp. 125, 159.

Interpreting the Doctrine
of the Incarnation
Richard A. Norris, Jr.

The question which we are to deal with at this conference has been defined for us by the titles of two recent English publications, one of which suggests that the notion of God incarnate is "myth," while the other insists that it is "truth." The issue, then, is which alternative is the correct one? Shall we call the doctrine of the Incarnation myth or truth?

I

I find this a very puzzling question. I do not think that myth and truth are necessarily opposites and, therefore, do not see why one must choose between them. A myth, after all, is a story; that is what the word means. A myth may, like the story of Odysseus and his wanderings, be essentially fictional and, in that sense, untrue. It may, on the other hand, like Plato's story of the creation of the world, be intended to state truth — and, indeed, truth of the deepest and most important sort. No doubt, if you had pressed Plato about his story, he would have admitted that it was not meant to be taken literally and that the truth it contained might be stated in a more direct way by speaking philosophically. At the same time, however, he would also have insisted that such a philosophical restatement might not, for many purposes, be the best way of presenting the truth which the myth contains. For story, after all, has its uses. It renders truth for us in a picture and so lets us grasp it imaginatively rather than abstractly; and at least in some circumstances that can be a manifest advantage.

If this is so, however, then to call the doctrine of the Incarnation myth is not, ipso facto, to insist that it conveys no truth.

Why, then, should we not say, and say unashamedly, that the doctrine of the Incarnation *is* myth, in the sense that it comes to us as a story which is not meant to be taken literally, but rather to be understood as intimating and conveying truth in an imaginative way?

That question is phrased in such a way as to demand an assenting answer. In fact, however, an assenting answer to it would be partly, at least, inappropriate; the doctrine of the Incarnation does not, in fact, come to us only in the form of myth. It comes to us in several forms; and the question of whether or not it presents itself as myth is one that has to be answered differently in the case of different historical sources.

Let us take an example: The very primitive statement of the doctrine in Philippians 2:5-11 is certainly myth, a myth whose imaginative and imaginal richness is so profound that it has been the source of theological and moral insight throughout the history of the Christian movement. Similarly, there are elements of myth in the way in which the Niceno-Constantinopolitan Creed states the doctrine. That creed speaks of one who is "true God" and describes this deity as "coming down," being "made flesh" and then dying and rising again. That is a story if ever I heard one; and it is a story which clearly intends to convey truth, even though one might stumble in understanding it if one insisted on the literal sense of every word it contains.

Alongside such statements of the doctrine, one must put others whose aim is to speak more directly and less figuratively — to recast the myth, so to speak, in more direct terms. Consider the case of St. Augustine. He tells the story of the Incarnation over and over again. At the same time, he takes great care to insist upon its limitations as an expression of the truth it seeks to tell. He is much troubled, for example, by the possible implications of a phrase like "came down from heaven." He is at some pains to point out in his treatise *On the Trinity* that the Incarnation of the Word of God does not mean an intervention in or invasion of the created order by a hitherto absent God — a God "up there" in heaven. On the contrary, he insists, God is always present everywhere for his people, as he is for the natural creation as a whole. The novelty of the Incarnation consists rather in the fact that it represents a new *mode* of God's presence. Thus he argues, in effect, that language about the Word of God's "coming down" needs to be interpreted; it is not meant literally, but has to be taken as "picture-language" appropriate to a story form.

In the same way, a multitude of other writers — writers who belonged to the age in which the form of the creeds was being fixed — spent a great deal of time pointing out that the expressions "became incarnate" and "became flesh" do not mean that God was turned into something else, as a frog might be turned into a prince. What these phrases mean, they argue, is that the Word of God somehow identified himself in and with a human life, all the while remaining what he always was and is.

Here, then, in the writings of the Church Fathers, we find the story of the Incarnation being told — and then being carefully explained in another mode of discourse. We find, if you like, both myth and demythologization. Consequently, we must acknowledge as historians that, while the doctrine of the Incarnation has been stated and will no doubt continue to be stated mythically, it may also be stated — and has also been stated — in other ways. Consider in this connection the case of the famous *Definition* of the Council of Chalcedon. That document, with all the piety one would expect of the fifth-century bishops who wrote it, presents itself as nothing more than a restatement of the Nicene Creed. In fact, though, where the creed speaks in story style, the *Definition* adopts a different kind of discourse. It offers, in effect, a model for christological language. That is, it tries to state the doctrine of the Incarnation by explaining how one ought to speak about the person of Christ. One must give an account of him, it says, in human terms, as a man. One must give an account of him as God-with-us. And one must do both of these things at the same time, without getting the two different accounts confused with each other.

If one can discover in the Chalcedonian *Definition* a document which treats the doctrine of the Incarnation in terms of what are essentially language rules, one can also find statements of it in positive metaphysical terms. Many of the Church Fathers sought to understand the Incarnation within the framework of a Neo-

platonist metaphysic. A modern theologian like Karl Rahner approaches it in the spirit of contemporary transcendental philosophy. We might debate which, if any, of these formulations is
most nearly adequate or correct; but, whether or not they
contain truth, they are certainly not mythic in form.

I would conclude, then, that *myth* is a word which aptly describes some statements of the doctrine of the Incarnation, but
not all. In arriving at this conclusion, however, we have opened
up an obvious and very basic problem. Our answer to the
question about myth has caused us to take note of something
which we sometimes suspect but seldom articulate: When we
glibly utter the phrase "doctrine of the Incarnation," it is not
easy to say precisely what we are referring to. Like a child posing
for a photographer, it wiggles as we try to get it set and in focus.
Do we mean the Nicene Council's formulation of the doctrine?
Do we mean Cyril of Alexandria's statement of it (not quite the
same thing)? Or do we mean the argument developed in, say,
Wolfhart Pannenberg's *Jesus, God and Man?* Where, to put it
bluntly, does one look to find this thing which we call "the
doctrine of the Incarnation"?

II

This issue is basic to our present discussion. We cannot know
what the debate is about or how to take the questions which are
being raised until we know what that phrase "doctrine of the Incarnation" denotes. What is more, an answer to this question
will do more than simply clear the ground for our thinking. It
will also — as I hope we shall see — contribute to a resolution of
the substantive issue about the status and meaning of the doctrine of the Incarnation. Let us take this question up, then, with
some care and caution.

What most people — at least casually and off-handedly —
take "doctrine of the Incarnation" to refer to is a particular, ver-
bally-formulated account of the person of Jesus, an account
which is lodged, so to speak, somewhere in the past. On this
point the different parties to the debate seem to agree. What they
differ on is the value or status which they would assign to the
doctrine thus located and defined. By one group, this past account of the person of Jesus is regarded as authoritative. Such

persons think that the business of the church today is to repeat, to reproduce without alteration of any sort, that understanding. Others, however, assert that it is impossible to reproduce or repeat this teaching, for, they point out, the very fact that it is lodged in the past — and so meshed into a thought-world which we can neither fully comprehend nor fully share — means that it is not really available to us. It cannot make sense to men and women who live, think and act on the basis of a set of assumptions about the world which are radically different from those which inform this traditional doctrine of the Incarnation.

In the light of the question we have raised and the observations which evoked it, it seems that a serious and fairly fundamental mistake is being made here. It requires only a moment's thought to realize that what is "lodged in the past" is not a single, uniform understanding of Jesus. On the contrary, it is a whole series of different — though not always or necessarily inconsistent — ways of understanding Jesus' relation to God and to us. But more than that, these differing christological formulations and images do not just lie there in the past separately like so many items in the window of an antique store. They stand, rather, in close historical relation to one another. Consider, as an example of what I mean, the christology of Nestorius. That account of Jesus, whatever one may think of it, is tied into a whole developing web of christological thought. It draws on the common tradition of the Church. It draws on the particular tradition of one school of thought. It is formed by its conscious opposition to an alternative tradition represented by Cyril of Alexandria. In short, it illustrates the fact that christologies grow in and out of one another, whether by way of development or by way of conflict. They are individual moments in a long, changing tradition of interpretation.

What this means, though, is that we must reexamine our natural assumption about what that phrase "doctrine of the Incarnation" refers to. It does not denote a uniform formula or a uniform understanding lodged somewhere in the past. Rather it denotes a continuous movement of thought, a dynamic with a particular logic and a particular focus. In other words, the doctrine of the Incarnation is a *process of interpretation,* one in which past experience and past understanding are at once preserved and transformed by being appropriated in the context of new questions and new ways of seeing things.

The picture, however, is even more complex than that. It is true, as I have said, that "new questions and new ways of seeing things" stimulate — and have stimulated — reconsideration of inherited christological ideas. It would be a mistake, however, to suppose that such reconsideration is brought about solely by the impact of external or secular changes on the Church's understanding of Christ. It is also brought about by problems and insights which have been created by the doctrine of the Incarnation itself. People's way of understanding Christ affects their understanding of themselves and their world; eventually it issues in new perspectives and insights which in turn demand that they change and deepen their way of appreciating Christ. When we say that the doctrine of the Incarnation has a dynamism about it, that it represents a *process* of interpretation, we do not merely mean that it gets changed as time goes on; we mean that it creates change, that it drives people to see things in new ways, and that among the things which thus get seen in new ways is that doctrine itself.

It seems to me, then, that the discussion we are engaged in is often conducted on a false assumption, one which in different ways vitiates the positions of both parties in the debate. On the one hand, to those who want to insist that the church's business is to say what it has always said, one must reply with an emphatic "Yes, but . . ." For the only way in which the church can say what it has always said is, paradoxically, by using its tradition to interpret and understand new situations — which, of course, entails letting those situations in turn interpret it. The result of such a procedure, however, cannot be a reproduction of the past (which, after all, has never really been reproduced or preserved by anyone). The result of such a policy is always change. From its Jewish tradition, the early Christian community drew the image of Messiah to interpret the phenomenon of Jesus. In this process it accomplished two things. It changed the meaning of Messiah by using it to characterize Jesus, for he filled the image with a new content. At the same time it changed its understanding of Jesus, for the symbol Messiah evoked appreciation of new dimensions of Jesus' person and work. And the same sort of thing will happen with us when we try to "preserve" our tradition. Should we seriously try to understand our experience as twentieth-century people in the light of images and ideas involved in the doctrine of God's incarnation in Christ, two things will inevitably happen: We will begin to see Christ in new ways and we will begin to experience our world in new ways. We will, in short, not reproduce the past but *interpret* it — which in fact is what we always do with it anyhow.

On the other hand, to those who want to insist that the idea of God's incarnation in Christ is simply lost in the past and incomprehensible, one must also reply with a "Yes, but . . ." To be sure, the past cannot simply be reproduced. At the same time, however, the past is vitally and organically connected with our present. It is not a distant, locked enclosure, an isolated little garden into which we curiously peer as over twenty-foot walls. It is not, to vary the metaphor, a box which is closed off and separate from that other box we call the present. For one thing, the world of thought and experience in which we live is a product of the past. It is, you might say, what the past has made of us. It is also true, however, that this world of ours represents what we make of the past. It is the product of our interpretation of the past — a projection of what the past means to us as we appropriate, repudiate and develop what it gives us. If, then, the doctrine of the Incarnation belongs to our past, what that means is not that it is inaccessible to us, that it has nothing to do with us, but on the contrary that it is one of the things which has made us who we are and therefore one of the things we will, and must, make something of.

Let us just say, then, that for us the doctrine of the Incarnation is a question, a question addressed by our past to our ways of thinking and valuing, to our ways of understanding ourselves. It is no light question though, no question which can easily be ignored; it challenges our "common sense," bound up as that is with the assumptions and attitudes of this present time and place. It represents a new possibility for our future, a suggestion that things may be different from what we ordinarily and naturally make of them. This is the way in which the doctrine of the Incarnation becomes an issue for us. It is not some neat formulation which we can either rest on or dismiss. It is a question which thrusts itself upon us and threatens to change our ways of seeing things, and therefore our ways of seeing ourselves.

If this is so, then we must ask, to begin with, not what the doctrine of the Incarnation says, but what the issues are with which it confronts us.

III

First, the doctrine of the Incarnation compels us to ask whether God is a serious issue for us. This may seem at first an eccentric way to phrase the question, but there is more to this formulation of the problem than meets the eye. The question is not whether or not one affirms the existence of some reality to which the label "God" can be attached. It is rather whether, as people struggle to come to terms with themselves and their world in practical ways, they understand that in their search for·meaning and coherence they are in fact asking about the ultimate meaning, the ultimate reason and the ultimate mystery of things. If they understand this, then God is an authentic issue for them — something real indeed, but real above all as a question, something about which they are sure and unsure at the same time. In such circumstances, God is an issue for them in the same way that they are an issue for themselves, as, in every word and action, they try to identify themselves in response to the demands and problems with which the world faces them.

And the point is that it was to people of this sort that Jesus proclaimed the Kingdom of God. His message was not for the righteous, for people who had or thought they had everything straight about themselves and about God. No, he spoke for sinners, for people who could claim very little in their lives that was neat and straight. To such people, God was overwhelmingly real — but real in the same way, perhaps, as he had been real for Job. They found God a source of simultaneous wonder and puzzlement, despair and hope. Like Job, they did not know quite what to make of him. Sometimes they wanted to nudge him into action; and sometimes they wanted to run from him. They stood before God as troubled questioners — unsure of him as they were unsure of themselves.

To people of this sort, Jesus came preaching that God himself was in process of setting things straight and that those who grasped the message must repent — change their minds, see themselves and God in a wholly new light. Jesus' ministry, then, was meant to be the instrument of a new relationship between God and God's people, a relationship in which things would at last be put right. On the one hand, that ministry signified God's identification of himself to people as the one who in the end really does set things straight, the one who graciously brings truth to light. On the other hand, it meant God's identification of human beings to themselves as the folk for and about whom this truth was told.

Here, I think, is the first question which the doctrine of the Incarnation puts to us. Are we people for whom a message of this sort is significant? Is God an issue for us in such a way that we see the meaning of our lives wrapped up in the questions who God is and what God is up to? If so, then we do not merely note the message of Jesus; we hear it. It meets us as the suggestion that a new life is possible.

Now a second question comes at us. Do we see that the message about God which Jesus bore is in the end coincident with his person — that, to phrase it straightforwardly, he *is* his message? Of course this is a state of affairs which does not always, or even normally, obtain. Postmen carry messages of whose burden they are not even aware. I can convey to someone a message whose content not only does not involve me, but is also, as a matter of fact, an affair of total indifference to me. On the other hand, if someone collapses on the street in front of me and I call for a doctor, the action I take means that I have, as they say, "got the message"; and the message in question cannot be distinguished from the unfortunate man or woman who called my action forth.

In the first instance, Jesus' message was conveyed by word and deed. All that he said and did was a signifying — a proclamation — of the Kingdom of God. At the same time, he was utterly and personally involved in this proclamation; and no doubt there were some people — his followers and disciples — who regarded him as the very embodiment of the message he bore. That, however, true though it be, is not the point to be made here. Our point is that, in the end, this message of Jesus' was most effectively delivered not so much by what he said and did as by the appearance of God's Kingdom in him — by people's experience of him as the one whom God raised to new life, the life of Coming Age. In the risen Jesus — and I take it that this is the whole point of the proclamation of the Resurrection — the Kingdom of God is discerned and the message about the Kingdom is delivered by being actualized. The person, then, truly becomes the message. Because this is so, believers begin to attach a whole range of honorific titles to Jesus. He is Messiah, Son of David — Son of God.

If we have got this far, though, a third question awaits us, one which cannot be avoided. Do we see and affirm that in this Christ — the one whose message about the Kingdom of God comes true in his person — our own relationship to God is not just revealed but determined? This is no light question; it needs a great deal more examination than we can give it now. One of its implications, however, is important for us here. The question suggests that the term "revelation," as we ordinarily use it, is inadequate for understanding the significance of Jesus. Jesus the Christ is not primarily one who, as we say, tells us something about God or shows us about God. That may be true enough as far as it goes; but if it is true, the reason is that this person whom we call "Lord and Christ" is the one who establishes and actualizes our proper identity before God and therefore, conversely, actualizes what God is for us. Jesus is not merely a clue to what we might reasonably mean by "God"; he is the determination, the realization, of what God means by *us*. This is what is implied by all the New Testament's talk about our being "in Christ," or our sharing in his death and resurrection, or our being branches of that Vine which he is. This is all, no doubt, very mysterious and figurative language; but what it seems to add up to is the idea that the Risen Christ defines what God is making of humanity so that, as people stand with him by faith, they "come to themselves," they appropriate and realize the identity which they have in God's eyes. If this is so, we have to say that the one in whose resurrection the Kingdom of God is actualized determines and constitutes our relation to God.

Then, finally, another question arises. If we say that Jesus the Christ is the determination of what we are to God, and so of what God is for us, then there is hardly any way in which we can avoid wondering whether this human being represents a definitive *gesture* of God in relation to us. What relates us to God can, in the last resort, only be God. To say this is not to formulate a statement of the doctrine of the Incarnation. It is merely to point to the problematic reality which has, historically, evoked the church's conviction about Jesus and to suggest that we too have to make some sense of it. Who but God can bring God's Rule? Who but God can say who we are, and are becoming, in God's purposes? It seems, therefore, that the least one can say about Jesus is that his humanity incorporates, represents, God in the act of being-for-us, because in him a real relationship is brought about between humanity and its Creator. That, at any rate, is the final issue with which the doctrine of the Incarnation confronts us; and it is not an unreal or insignificant issue merely because the historical source of it lies in a past era which habitually saw and explained things in a way different from ours.

IV

It must be very clear, however, that anyone who asks these four questions and wants, or suspects that he wants, to answer them in the affirmative will have a multitude of problems on his hands. These problems, moreover, will be of a very serious order, because they will have to do with our way of understanding and talking about God.

For example, the Church's talk of Incarnation clearly insists that God objectifies himself for us in the life and death and new life of one human being. The Mystery of all being, it says, the Context and Ground of everything that is, focuses itself as love for us in one human being. Do we not run the risk, though, in such assertions as these, of forgetting that it really is *God* we are talking about? To be sure, this problem arises in connection with any language which identifies or associates the Ultimate —

God — with ordinary events or things in our experience; but it raises its head with particular vigor when the problem of the Incarnation is being discussed. How can the Transcendent, the Universal, the Ground of absolutely everything which is, be known as a particular thing or person within the created order? How can God be in some sense "then" and now "now"; Semitic and not Indo-European; male and not female; Jesus and not Peter or Paul or you or me? Surely God, who is intimately and universally present as the loving sustainer of all things, cannot be particularized or, as it were, localized.

On the other hand, if God were related in absolutely the same way to everything, he would make no difference. He would, as we say, be a constant factor, a mere symbol for the established and unchanging framework of things. The trouble is, though, that we only know and respond to things and so enter into conscious relation with them in terms of the differences they make, that is, in terms of the way they stand out from other things or occasion change in the way things are. If, then, we are to know and relate ourselves to God at all, God must be and do something "different" and particular in our world. The universal Ground of all, ingredient in every event, must nevertheless be known specifically and particularly through events, things and persons which have definite character, which embody or make a "difference."

The fact that this is so, however, need not mean either that God "intervenes" in the world (as though he were normally "out of it" altogether) or that God literally becomes, or turns himself into, an item in our world. Maybe we can say (to return to a phrase I used earlier) that God *objectifies himself* for people in and through particular worldly realities. If we choose language of this sort, however, then we will have to beware of popular confessional statements like "Jesus is God," which can be, to put it as mildly as possible, dangerously misleading. The trouble with such statements, of course, is that in fact they do seem simply to identify God as a particular intraworldly reality — in this case, a specific human person. To make such an identification, though, is not to state but to miss the point of the church's teaching about Jesus. For classical statements about the Incarnation begin with the assumption that God is anything but a particular human being. He is, on the contrary, the transcendent divine "other" who, in the Incarnation, remains just that. By the same token, the Church's tradition wants to insist that Jesus really is a human being — an *ordinary* human being like us. To say "the Word was made flesh," then, refers not to a simple identity of God and Jesus but to a relationship in which God lovingly identifies himself in and with a real human person, so that that person can truly be called the Word, the self-communication and self-objectification of God in human terms.

The question is: Can this be said intelligibly? The church fathers, with their doctrine of two distinct but unified natures in Christ, tried to say it. They were entirely clear in their minds that one must not "confuse" God with a human being. Somehow, they thought, it must be possible to understand Jesus as one in whom God and humanity are entirely at one and yet remain essentially different from each other. In attempting to say, this, however, they got themselves into a great deal of trouble by their use of that word *nature*. Consider, after all, what it might mean to speak of a divine nature in contrast to a human nature. Does it mean that the two are comparable but contrary like, say, apple-nature and grape-nature? If so, then presumably God and humanity must somehow exist on the same plane. They must be, as it were, different items in a single list, just as apple and grape name different items in a list of fruits. In this view, Jesus would have to be something like a cross between deity and humanity; or perhaps a mixture of them.

This obviously will not do, simply because the word *God* is not the name of a nature in the sense intended. We can speak of human nature, meaning something like "that which is normally characteristic of all human beings"; and we can contrast this human nature with that of other animate and inanimate creatures. God, however, is beyond these differences of nature because he is the source and ground of all of them. He is not different from human beings in the way, say, that a wolf or cactus plant is different from a human being. He is different in the sense that he does not belong within the framework which allows such beings to be compared and contrasted with one another. On the contrary, he is the very source of the framework, the "beyond" which is the context of its being.

If that is so, however, if the divine nature is in fact not a nature at all, but the Beyond which grounds and nurtures all natures, maybe the idea of the Incarnation is not as senseless as traditional formulations have sometimes made it appear. There is a difference between being God and being human; but the difference is not an incompatibility in the way that being an apple and being a grape are incompatible. If the ultimate reality which we call God is the ground and perfector of human nature, and not a competitor with it, then it is not inconceivable that God can be with people in and as a human person — and that without its being thought that God has turned into something other than what he is.

I began these remarks by saying that the doctrine of the Incarnation has its roots in the question of God and of people's relation to God as the ultimate mystery of things. I would like to close by coming back to that point for, while the debate we are carrying on has its focus in historical formulations of the doctrine of the Incarnation, what it is really concerned with in the final analysis is the question of what we mean by God — whether it makes sense to believe and to say that the ultimate mystery of things is a mystery of the self-communication of love in truth. If we conceive of God as some ultimate which just lies around providing a certain order to things, then the doctrine of the Incarnation cannot make much sense. That sort of God is a presupposition of our thought, not a real "other" who knows us, gives himself to be with us and evokes our trust and love. It is the latter sort of God, however, which the doctrine of the Incarnation in all its varied — adequate and inadequate — formulations proclaims. Somehow, the value of Jesus in Christian experience has been the value of "God with us"; and the point of that lies not only in what it says about Jesus, but also, and primarily, in what it says about God. The trouble is that apart from Jesus — from what he said and did and what happened to him — we might not have the courage to speak of "God with us." That is why the story of Jesus, and the account of him as Word made flesh, are not and cannot be, for us, *mere* story, but must always be story which catches us, for all our modernity, right between wind and water — right where we are secretly wondering about God.

Jesus as Savior and Lord   *Roy I. Sano*

Introduction

I am grateful for the privilege to participate in this National Conference of the Trinity Institute West. It is appropriate that a member of an ethnic minority makes one of the presentations. This session is conducted in a state which the lieutenant governor's office predicted will be a "Third World" state by the year 1990.[1] That is, in about a decade the colorful people will outnumber whites in the most populous state of the Union.

I am cognizant that I, as an Asian American, come from one of California's smaller ethnic groups — we are considerably fewer in number than Hispanics or Blacks. But it may be fitting at this western regional conference for an Asian American to offer a statement. Proportionately speaking, we are the most rapidly growing ethnic minority group in the United States, having grown by 55% in the 1960s and possibly growing by 75-85% in the 1970s. Furthermore, 70% of us live in the western states.

One might note that this session takes place in an area where people are increasingly facing the Pacific Ocean and Asia, with their backs to Europe and the Atlantic Ocean much of the time.

---

[1] As quoted by Clifford Alika, *Ethnic Minority Population: A Demographic Study for the Task Force on Strengthening the Ethnic Minority Local Church* (Berkeley, California: The California-Nevada Conference of the United Methodist Church, 1977), referring to *California Manpower Indicators from the 1970 Census, Summary Manpower Indicators,* published by the State of California, Department of Human Resources Development, Employment Data and Research (July 1972), Sacramento, California.

This is understandable, if the predictions of the Anglican missionary historian, Stephen Neill, are true. In his book *Colonialism and Christian Mission,*[2] he predicted that the Pacific Ocean will become the fourth center of world history. With a Euro-American bias, he says that humanity has lived with its center in the Tigris-Euphrates valley, then the Mediterranean and, most recently, in the Atlantic. The next stage of human history will center in the Pacific.

Given these considerations, my presentation has been prepared from the perspective of an Asian American living on the Pacific Coast. My sketch of a part of that perspective for our understanding of Jesus will follow a familiar series of considerations. Christians have frequently come to their understanding of Jesus through their experience of salvation. In turn, their view of salvation is shaped by their struggles against sin and evil. Thus, my presentation will move from a consideration of sin and evil to an interpretation of salvation and will conclude with a reformulation of Christology. Only at that point will it be evident how a Pacific and Asian American perspective is related to the topic, "The Myth/Truth of the God Incarnate."

Sin and Evil in Human Rights Struggles

Liberation theologians have called for critical reflection on praxis. While the Pacific and Asian American communities are engaged in a variety of efforts, I will use two incidences related to their human rights struggles as samples of a praxis which illuminates our reflections.

Incidences: In 1973, the officers of the Pacific and Asian American Center for Theology and Strategies (PACTS), based in Berkeley, California, asked a Filipino American minister for assistance. Since he was returning for a visit to the Philippines, he was asked to consult with leaders in the human rights struggles of that country. It was agreed that, when he came back to the

---

[2]Stephen Neill, *Colonialism and Christian Mission* (London: Lutterworth, 1966).

United States, he would itinerate in churches and community groups and report on the latest developments. After his visit abroad, he notified PACTS that he could not itinerate. His ailing father had made him promise that he would not make public the disturbing occurrences under President Ferdinand Marcos. His father insisted that actions taken in the United States by his son would only prompt reprisals on relatives living in the Philippines. Subsequent events have confirmed his prediction.

One such confirmation occurred in 1978. Seven persons in the Anti-Martial Law Coalition visited the Philippine consulate in San Francisco on April 13, 1978. They requested that the officials in charge deliver a message to President Marcos in Manila, denouncing the sham national election of the week before. They also demanded the release of 600 members of the opposition party who had been imprisoned following the election and the termination of martial law. In the midst of the ensuing altercations, one consulate official threatened a member of the delegation, a Filipino immigrant who had become a naturalized United States citizen: "Why are you doing this? You know that we can 'take care' of your relatives in the Philippines." On September 11, 1978, her uncle in the Philippines was found floating in a river, supposedly dead from drowning. An autopsy report arranged by relatives revealed two days later that he had died from strangulation. The man's son went underground the day his father was found.

Dimensions of Sin and Evil: Comparable incidences among Formosans, Koreans and, earlier, Indochinese living in the United States can be cited. At least three levels of issues have become evident to us. We are very clearly encountering the actions of specific officers and agents, and their effects on individuals concern us. The arrest and torture of public figures such as Trinidad Herrera in Manila and the imprisonment of the Reverend Ms. Cho, Hwa-Soon in Seoul prompt actions directed toward individuals. Protests are lodged with the offenders, support is mobilized for the victims. But, to state the obvious, the systemic dimensions behind these isolated events become conspicuous as we contest individual officers. The global institutions and networks represent the second level of the issues confronted in human rights struggles. Within the countries abroad, we are faced with a neo-feudalism where an elite within a given nation is capable of gaining control over the economy, the legislative assemblies and judicial systems, as well as the police and military forces. These ruling elites work out arrangements with countries such as ours to further their ends. The familiar pattern of arrangements include the invitation of United States-based multinational corporations, as well as the back-up systems of our armed forces and intelligence. Educational, cultural and religious institutions frequently add their sanctions.

However, the familiar practice of identifying and analyzing the systemic and institutional factors which contribute to the violation of human rights is not sufficient. It overlooks the third element, which coalesces what it is that we confront and gives it the momentum it has manifested. Ideologies and an ethos are at work. They are expressed in such words as *Westernization, modernization, development, growth* and *national security.* These terms are not abstractions. They summarize, like laws and principles, the patterns of arrangements and the courses of events which operate in and through institutions and systems. They virtually convert people into puppets and make specific practices very predictable.

Introducing "national security" considerations into the implementation of foreign policies can lead the president of the United States to kill the "soul" of his proposals for human rights. Legislative investigations can be terminated when national security considerations are invoked. The National Security Council represents one of the highest decision-making bodies in this nation. Thus, the total vision of the combatant we encounter in our efforts to foster human rights includes specific individuals and global institutions, all combined into an organic network infused with an ideology. Although we cannot speak simply in monolithic terms, the various components work with sufficient coordination so that an organic ascription is not an exaggeration. We find ourselves rehabilitating the ancient symbol systems which mention the demonic and the satanic elements which can operate through individuals, institutions and ideologies. The interplay of all three makes the pervasive schizophrenic analysis of sin and evil into either personal or social terms look very misleading.

Although the effective operations of the network requires the willing cooperation from people abroad, the ideology and ethos are "Made in the U.S.A." and exported abroad. The ethos has grown over the centuries, but in the last three decades the legitimacy and nobility of the rhetoric blinded us to their demonic uses. We sought recovery from war-time devastation which others suffered; we promoted modernization for the less developed. We created alliances for the national securities of people so that they could be protected against others who would disrupt these noble ambitions. And at home we sought further growth beyond our affluence. As we pursued these ends, we elevated to an extraordinary prestige and power those forces which would accomplish these goals. To mention them again, they include multinational corporations, intelligence networks, military alliances and the cultural pursuits through research and educational institutions, as well as religious bodies. These agencies for modernization, development, national security and growth have become the "hosts of lords" which have exploited and repressed, corroded and oppressed. Without sufficient checks on the exercise of their mandates, they have overreached their charters and become "principalities and powers" whereby contradicting God's intention for all creatures, both human and natural. They have violated the fulfillment of human potential God has willed. What we have exported abroad has come home to roost. Thus, we see international networks coordinate actions abroad with those at home. They have called into being makeshift networks among East Asians and Asian Americans who seek to mitigate the adverse effects of these principalities and powers.

Although the violations cut across the Marxist, Maoist and capitalist ideologies, the words of Jesus challenge us to address those which primarily originate from within our own society: ". . . first take the log out of your own eye, and then you will see clearly to take the speck out of your brother's eye" (Matthew 7:5).

Biblical Analysis: Because the economic, political, military, social and cultural issues are profoundly real on their own terms, they have been permeated with religious and spiritual concerns. How this has happened requires some elaboration. In broad outlines, the biblical mythologies themselves have helped us uncover the religious and spiritual issues involved in apparently secular problems. It will not be necessary to show the full range of spiritual issues which reside in social concerns. The presence of such basic considerations as what it is we trust and what it is that evokes awe, will have to suffice for this presentation.

We came to see that recognizing and doing battle against something more than individuals was not our invention. Early Christians had an analogous perception. Although the Apostle Paul, being the good Jew that he was, affirmed the existence of one God, his experiences led him into an acknowledgement of intermediaries between God and humankind. "For although there may be so-called gods in heaven or on earth — as indeed there are many 'gods' and many 'lords,' — yet for us there is one God, . . . and one Lord, Jesus Christ . . ." (1 Corinthians 8:5-6).

In Ephesians, we do not only have a neutral acknowledgement of their existence, but a moral evaluation of this second order of reality. "We are not contending against flesh and blood, but against the principalities, against the powers, against the world rulers of this present darkness" (Ephesians 6:12).

These references might be used to depict the systemic qualities of institutional arrangements which we found ourselves struggling against. But the same passage permits us to see the way institutions and ideologies are intertwined. In recognition of the illusive but real qualities which the ideological enemies of humanization can have, the ancient writer referred to them as "spiritual hosts of wickedness in the heavenly places" (Ephesians 6:12).

A more directly useful figure of speech appears in Paul's letter to the Galatians. When he wrote that they had been enslaved by the "elemental spirits of the universe," he articulated the capacities of an ideology and an ethos to gain control over societies and manipulate the lives of people (Galatians 4:3, 8, 9).

The Apostle Paul's teaching concerning the law casts further light upon the oppressive powers which an ethos can exercise. For him, the law summarized the genius of the ancient religion of his ancestors. It represented a gift of God to the children of Israel. Although he wrote that the law is "holy and just and good" (Romans 7:12), Paul also recognized the curse it could inflict (Galatians 3:13). Under the influence of the Protestant Reformers, our interpretation of Paul's attack on the law have been turned into a general rejection of any moral standard as a condition for salvation. By generalizing the point Paul made, we overlook the potential for contemporary implications of the historical context in which he originally announced salvation by grace through faith. The law he had in mind represented a revelation of God appropriate to a particular people within their unique history. As such it was good. But when the summary of that form of life was applied without adaptation to all people regardless of their history, culture or place, it became an instrument of death (Romans 4:15). Genuine salvation would not come by observing the law which was alien to a people, but it could come by means of liberation from that law (Romans 10:4). Though subsequent extension of this Reformation teaching concerning salvation without the works of the law may be sound, we should not overlook the original ethnic and cultural setting.

Just as Paul saw the genius of his own people could become 'an elemental spirit of the universe" that could enslave people, we have come to see how destructive our ideologies can become, regardless of the genius behind them or the good intentions which created them. While our ideology can operate as a "word of life" in one setting, they can become the "letter of the law" which spells out a sentence of death in another context (2 Corinthians 3:6; Romans 7:6).

If this reinterpretation of the biblical references to the intermediaries and the law helped us see that we were not alone in doing battle with institutions and ideologies, the biblical view of idolatry helped us see the issue of sin as integral to these evils. The early Christians recognized with the ancient Hebrews the critical place idolatry had. "You shall have no other gods before me" (Exodus 20:3) was the first among the summary of God's commands. In Paul's analysis of sin and evil, the critical human error came when they "exchanged the glory of the immortal God for" various duplicates (Romans 1:23). "Since they did not see fit to acknowledge God, God gave them up to a base mind and to improper conduct. They were filled with all manner of wickedness, evil, covetousness, malice . . . envy, murder, strife, deceit . . ." (Romans 1:28-29). In the Fourth Gospel, the writer has Jesus speak in pastoral words the same message. He says, we will find all others besides the Good Shepherd are thieves, who rob, kill, and destroy (John 10:10) when we allow them to shepherd us.

It has been the contention of this analysis that our ideologies and institutions, the ethos and networks, have turned into gods who are asked to shepherd us into the promised land. That subtle but pervasive idolatry among the unchurched and the most pious and law-abiding Christians has produced frightening consequences which reach across the waters and call us into mission.

Breaking through the Modern Blinders: Before leaving this analysis of sin and evil, a word must be said about the three-storied worldview, with God, humankind and the intervening second orders of realities. This outlook sounds outdated and probably paranoid to many. A number of factors are at work which makes such an analysis sound so foreign to us. First, our scientism has depopulated the cosmos of anything other than natural forces which we can understand and master, and our own actions. Second, our humanism and individualism foreclose any recognition of powers which could have sway over us. Third, and perhaps most important of all, is the class bias which makes the world look different. As heirs of the revolutions from the seventeenth through the nineteenth centuries, all the intermediaries between God and humankind such as the royalty, nobility and clergy seem to be overthrown or domesticated. Thus, if scientism made us dull-witted and unimaginative in reading the Bible, our pride and class bias blinded us from seeing any value in the grand drama of salvation in the Bible which recognizes "hosts of lords" who could manipulate us. Those bib lical stories, such as the apocalyptic ones, looked like the bizarre creation of deranged minds. Though the uses of these stories involve abuses, as any part of the Bible does, we overlooked the positive uses faithful Christians had made with them in history.[3] The Koreans, for example, under the Japanese occupation of their peninsula (1895-1945), found the Book of Daniel and the Apocalypse so inspiring that the Japanese colonial government eventually prohibited reading or preaching from them. Recent studies also have revealed the constructive role apocalypticism has played in United States civil religion and reform movements.[4]

We are learning that, if we do theology from the so-called "underside," the world and the Bible can look different to us. We come to see the emergence of new principalities and powers, and we hear God calling to be in mission against usurpers to God Almighty, even if they are our benefactors, our ideologies and our institutions. The bungling and destructive reign of the pretenders to the Almighty have helped us hear that biblical witness of faithful Christians.

---

[3]See, for example, Norman Cohn, *The Pursuit of the Millennium: Revolutionary Millenarians and Mystical Anarchists of the Middle Ages,* revised and expanded edition (New York: Oxford University Press, 1970) and Rosemary Radford Ruether, *The Radical Kingdom: The Western Experience of Messianic Hope* (New York: Paulist Press, 1970). Jaroslav Pelikan traces the persistence of the apocalyptic perspective in his study of *The Christian Tradition: A History of the Development of Doctrine, Volume I, The Emergence of the Catholic Tradition (100-600)* (Chicago: The University of Chicago Press, 1971) noting its virility long after the so-called "delay of the parousia" which played a crucial role for such historians as Martin Werner in his *Die Entstehung des christlichen Dogmas problemgeschichtlich dargestellt* (Bern, 1941).

[4]See Cushing Strout's survey of the longstanding tradition of the uses of apocalypticism in the United States civil religion in his book *The New Heavens and New Earth: Political Religion in America* (New York: Harper & Row, 1974). The seventeenth and eighteenth centuries are surveyed in Nathan O. Hatch's *The Sacred Cause of Liberty: Republican Thought and Millennium in Revolutionary New England* (New Haven: Yale University Press, 1977) and James W. Davidson's *The Logic of Millennial Thought: Eighteenth-Century New England* (New Haven: Yale University Press, 1977). The earlier study by Ernest Lee Tuveson, *Redeemer Nation: The Idea of America's Millennial Role* (Chicago: The University of Chicago Press, 1968) covers the nineteenth century in the main and takes account of the constructive and negative uses of apocalypticism.

Salvation as Redemption

If the central focus for an analysis of sin and evil rests on the theme of domination of destructive powers, then the emphasis in our understanding of salvation is naturally placed on deliverance from these powers. The contemporary word for deliverance or redemption is *liberation*. This vision of salvation should be distinguished from recent emphases characteristic of United States Protestantism. The mainline Protestants have lived with four "Rs" in their view of salvation and the mission of the church. In the 1950s, after World War II, we wanted renewal; in the 1960s, after the emergence of new movements, we wanted relevance; and in the 1970s, after a decade of polarization, we wanted reconciliation. Evangelicals and fundamentalists remained loyal throughout to their own sacred words. They called for regeneration and prayed for revivals.

Despite these distinctive emphases in the recent decades by United States Protestantism, it stands heir most of all to that overwhelming influence of European Christianity which interpreted salvation almost exclusively in terms of reconciliation, including justification and sanctification. Ever since the early Middle Ages, after the church came to terms with the Roman Empire, we became concerned with reconciliation. I would hazard a historical guess that the hankering for reconciliation with the persecuting Roman Empire became the paradigm for salvation. Although there is evidence in the pre-Constantine church for a yearning for liberation from the domination of principalities and powers, they also sought peace with the political powers and read that concern into their relations with God, their relations among humankind and within individual persons.

A look at the interpretations for the work of Jesus illustrates the point. Gustav Aulen demonstrated decades ago in his book *Christus Victor*[5] that the pre-Constantinian Christians such as Irenaeus and Origen thought of Jesus as a redeemer who delivered us from the clutches of demonic powers. The undetected

---

[5]Gustav Aulen, *Christus Victor: An Historical Study of the Three Main Types of the Idea of Atonement,* translated by A. G. Hebert, reprinted with an introduction by Jaroslav Pelikan (New York: Macmillan, 1969).

implication of his study should be noted. When the church no longer lived under the domination of imperial Rome, it saw Jesus as reconciler. Two chief interpretations of Jesus and his work came later in the Middle Ages. They depicted Jesus restoring right relations between God and humankind, either through the moral theory of Abelard or the legal views of Anselm. Liberation or redemption from oppression receded into the background; reconciliation upstaged redemption. What liberation theology challenges us to do is to restore a fuller drama of salvation. We can see now how redemption provides the condition for self-respecting and authentic reconciliation. The other "Rs" — regeneration, revivals, renewal, relevance — have their place as well, but assume subordinate roles within the larger drama of salvation.

We in the United States should appreciate that sequence which moves from redemption to reconciliation, since we find that pattern among our most cherished myths which define our identity and mission. For example, in the seventeenth century the Pilgrims came out from under what they saw as tyranny in England in order to create a new community. Notice, first the exodus or liberation from England, then the Mayflower Compact before they would step foot on New England soil. Later, in our myth of origins as a nation, the Declaration of Independence of 1776 announced our intentions of overthrowing what was seen as the manipulations of an unrepresentative Parliament. The colonists saw in the Revolutionary War a new exodus, a movement away from the exploitation and domination of powers who had alien interests. Only later was it possible to create a new community with the Constitution of 1789. Thus, in the two cycles of our myth of origins, we replay the same drama of salvation, first redemption and then reconciliation.[6]

Our attachment to reconciliation tempts Third World Christians to look upon us as God looked upon ancient Israel. Our desire for peace with God and harmony with our neighbor, our re-

---

[6]My attempt at a liberation theology for white middle-class people in the United States experimented with a sketch of this view. See, Roy I. Sano, *You Can Be Set Free* (Nashville, Tennessee: The United Methodist Publishing House/The Graded Press, 1977), pp. 8-12.

duction of salvation to reconciliation in our theology of salvation or in our celebration of the Eucharist, could all come under
the strictures recalled by Amos.

> I hate, I despise your feasts, and I take no delight in your solemn
> assemblies. Even though you offer me your burnt offerings and
> cereal offerings, I will not accept them, and the peace offerings of
> your fatted beasts I will not look upon. Take away from me the
> noise of your songs; . . . But let justice roll down like waters and
> righteousness like an ever-flowing stream (Amos 5:21-24).

Before we appreciate the legitimate place liberation has in the
story of salvation, we will need to recognize that we are indeed
under the domination of powers. That presents a difficulty when
the seat of imperialism is said to be in this country. Even if we
acknowledge that much of the problems originate here, we may
be reluctant to appreciate the perspective of Third World peoples who see us living under the domination of those powers
which outmaneuver others. In our pride we are likely to feel we
can still bring those rulers into line. For example, the middle
class, which holds the upper hand in theological education, or
the pulpiteers, who publish their sermons, still believe they are
within earshot of those who control this nation and that they can
introduce sufficient changes which do not require major altera-
tions in our society. No wonder they appeal to the model of
prophets who stood before kings and counseled correctives.
They recall Nathan before King David, Amos before Jeroboam,
Jesus before Pilate, and Paul before Roman officials. But they
overlook the apocalyptic dimensions of prophetism, or the way
apocalypticism replaced the prophets. In the last years of their
nationhood, the prophets turned apocalyptic when evils endured
despite amendments to the contrary. Eventually, when the people of Israel became vassals under alien peoples, the apocalyptic
orientation came into its own. The people of God needed redemption from the hold evil forces had upon them. They
dreamed of God overturning demonic forces and reestablishing
rulership over them, as Third World theologians at home and
abroad can be heard to say.

Although many liberation theologians look to the exodus as

the model for salvation, this analysis of salvation has sought to place that event in the context of a fuller story of salvation which moves from exodus to the covenant at Sinai. In this way, it has formulated a story of salvation which moves from redemption to reconciliation. The discussion has also introduced apocalyptic stories as another source for a model of liberation. They suggest the need for a major alteration in the power arrangements in the world so that people may be freed from the domination of destructive powers.

The Reigning One Redeems

If our fallen state is seen primarily in terms of oppression and our view of salvation restores the place redemption should have, then it should be clear why the focus shifts from Jesus as reconciler or mediator to Jesus as redeemer. The meaning of the redeemer, or savior, is best understood through a restatement of the lordship of Jesus. In broad outlines, as Jesus becomes the Lord of Hosts over the "hosts of lords," he will save us from oppression and exploitation which the principalities and powers can inflict. The one who reigns, therefore, is the one who redeems. A restatement of the way Jesus becomes Lord, and will become the full Prevailer, will spell that out more adequately.

As we worked with Christians involved in liberation struggles, one clear message from the apocalyptic tradition became evident: Evil forces have been disarmed. That is why they are courageous enough to engage the destructive powers. The writer of Colossians stated it well. "He [Jesus] disarmed the principalities and powers and made a public example of them, triumphing over them in him" (Colossians 2:15).

The religious rhetoric, however, should not blind us to the persisting strength of disarmed powers. We live in what has been called the "time between the times," which suggests three times — one each at the beginning and at the end, with another time in between. We might speak of the three phases of the lordship of Jesus, or stages in which Jesus is Prevailer, to experiment with the translation of the Greek *kurios* and the Hebrew *yahweh tsebaoth*. A reformulation of these times will state the identity of Jesus which sustains people in their struggles.

First, the time at the beginning is that moment when Jesus disarmed the principalities and powers, culminating in the event of the cross. During his life, the teachings and deeds of Jesus, such as his exorcism and healing, are seen as intrusions into and a takeover of the "territory" previously occupied by the Evil One. It was as if the Evil One mounted a last-ditch stand and hurled the full armaments at his disposal against Jesus on the cross and succeeded in slaying him (Mark 3:27; Luke 11:21-23).

Anyone who lives with such trust and vulnerability in faithful service to the living God becomes the avenue of new work. God overcame death in Jesus and raised him from the hold which death had. Thus, in the Crucifixion and Resurrection Jesus has "already" become the Lord. The first of the times, therefore, is called the "already" of Jesus as the Lord and Prevailer (Philippians 2:5-11).

There is a second time, sometimes called the "time between the times." People speak of it as the "not yet," because the lordship or reign of Jesus is "not yet" fully established. In the symbolism of the biblical story, the beast suffers a mortal wound but paradoxically is healed (Revelation 13:12). In a comparable vision, and probably its actual origins, the Book of Daniel depicts a time when "the beast was slain, and its body destroyed and given over to be burned with fire. As for the rest of the beasts, their dominion was taken away, but their lives were prolonged for a season and a time" (Daniel 7:11-12).

Thus, we characterize our time today as a period when Jesus is "not yet" fully Lord or Prevailer. In the Resurrection Jesus has already inflicted the mortal wounds upon those who would tyrannize humankind; he has already taken away the dominion of the "host of lords." But the wounded beasts can flail about and inflict injury; the dethroned resist the end of their reign and create havoc.

Christians, however, look forward to a third time. I suggest we designate it as the "then," which follows the "already" and thee "not yet." Paul writes the Corinthians, saying "*Then* comes the end, when he delivers the kingdom to God . . . after destroying every rule and every authority and power. For he must reign until he has put all his enemies under his feet" (1 Corinthians 15:24-25; italics added).

Or, returning to the drama of salvation as the Seer recorded it in the Apocalypse, there will come a time when we will hear it sung: "The kingdom of the world has become the kingdom of our Lord and of his Christ, and he shall reign for ever and ever" (Revelation 11:15).

A contemporary rewriting of these lines might read as follows. When Jesus destroys the reign of evil operating through economic, military, intelligence and cultural networks we have created, *then* it will be wholly appropriate to speak of Jesus as Lord.

Because theological formulation of this sort can be abstract, I will offer two ways we might make this story more concrete. They answer two questions: What are we trying to do in mission and what are we doing in the Eucharist?

When we speak of making Jesus Lord of Hosts over the hosts of lords, our mission and ministry could mean we are called to facilitate the reign of the Compassionate One over the reign of terror which prevails wherever we support martial law regimes. We are called to promote the reign of the Prince of Peace over the understandable animosities which exploitations provoke in millions of workers around the globe, the reign of the God of truth over the censorship which peddles lies and the media which converts our ethos into laws for others. With this narrative of salvation we can promote the reign of the One who is Whole, or Holy, over the rampant filth in shantytowns and the diseases impairing children for life. Thus, as Jesus reigns as the Lord of Hosts over the hosts of lords, we are redeemed from sin and evil. As we facilitate the reign of the Prevailer over the principalities and powers, we are liberated from their destructive domination. As Jesus becomes Lord he also becomes Savior; the One who reigns is the Redeemer.

If that is the missional implications of the christological formulation of Jesus as Savior and Lord, there are liturgical implications as well. In celebrating the Eucharist with prisoners and former prisoners of conscience, I became aware of the idolatry which remains unchallenged in our eucharistic theology. There was a time when we learned to distinguish between the Kingdom of God and the church in theology, and thus undercut a strong underpinning for triumphalism and idolatry in our ecclesiology. Involvements in liberation movements have taught me to speak of the Absence of Christ alongside the Presence of Christ in the Eucharist as a way of avoiding idolatry at a sacrosanct moment in our lives. As we sang the hymns, as the preacher proclaimed the word, and as the celebrant invited us to "take, eat . . . drink" I heard the ancient confession of the early church. "Jesus Christ is Lord." But when we prayed, and men wept for their children, spouses and parents who remained outside the prisons, I heard another word. They cried, "Our Lord, Come" (1 Corinthians 16:22; Revelation 22:20b).

As they helped me enter into the living reality of the ancient biblical confesion that Jesus is Lord and that ancient cry, "Come, Lord," so too reflections on that experience helped me uncover a witness of the early church which I had not noticed. Not only did the early church proclaim the Presence of Jesus in the Eucharist, they gave witness to the Parousia — the coming not yet realized. Luke recalls Jesus saying at the last supper that he would not eat or drink with his disciples until the reign of God had been established. "I shall not eat it until it is fulfilled in the reign of God. . . . for I tell you that from now on I shall not drink of the fruit of the vine until the reign of God comes" (Luke 22:16, 18: Matthew 26:29; Mark 14:25).

Even if we say Jesus is present as the host, the passage suggests he will not join us in the supper. Is that not what we find again in Luke 24 in the story of the disciples on the road to Emmaus? He opened the Scriptures, broke bread, but left without eating. Some such story was needed to depict the juxtaposition of the confession with the cry, the Presence with the Absence.

Paul had his way of affirming the absence. He said, in the memorial "You proclaim the Lord's death until he comes" (1 Corinthians 11:26), as if the full presence will not be realized until some future moment. If the *locus classicus* for the Presence of Christ in the Eucharist appears in the doctrine of Transubstantiation of the elements for the medieval church, the *locus classicus* for Presence in recent decades has been placed in the act of memorial, of *anamnesis.* In the very passage, however, where the Presence by memorial is affirmed, Paul asserts what I suggest we call the Absence of Christ.

Recently, we emphasized doing theology as story or narrative. The story implicit in the Apostles' Creed affirms his absence in the Ascension and his coming again. In the eucharistic memorial acclamation, we assert, "Christ has died, Christ is risen, Christ will come again," as if to imply an absence. Thus, the biblical and theological heritage suggests a corrective to our idolatrous eucharistic theology which only affirms the Presence of Christ, without recognizing the absence implied in the Parousia of Christ. The people who immerse themselves in liberation struggles can facilitate the recovery of that neglected heritage. Many of us found ourselves in the racial revolutions in the United States singing, "Kumbaya, my Lord" — translated, we are told, "Come by here, my Lord." We also learned to sing, "We shall overcome," not "We have overcome." What I am now saying is that the courageous Christians in Asia have taught me the same point. Confessing Jesus is Lord can be conjoined with a cry, "Come, Lord." We need those who have known prisons and the filth of hovels to teach us what T. S. Eliot said the Magi experienced when they saw the Lord Almighty born helpless in the stench of a stable: "We returned to our places, these Kingdoms/ No longer at ease here, in the old dispensation,/ With an alien people clutching their gods."

Therefore, let not the holy moment of the Eucharist when we affirm the presence of the Lord turn into idolatry or sanction of the status quo. Recall all those moments in biblical history when the cry of the oppressed mobilized God into a liberating action, and calls us into the same mission. The missional and eucharistic implications of the lordship of Jesus will illustrate the claim that the One who reigns redeems. As Jesus becomes the Lord of Hosts over the hosts of lords, we will be liberated from the destructive domination, the demonic abuses, of principalities and powers. Without that salvation, our hankering for reconciliation is diversionary, a sentimental but nonetheless insidious theology of oppression. Some such articulation of our Christology can help us make sense out of that lived reality we encounter in those who struggle for human rights. Thanks be to God for their gift to us. Praises be to God for the reigning One who redeems, that living Lord of Hosts who saves, even our faithful brother, Jesus! Amen.

Conclusion

A question remains: How is this analysis of sin and evil, the salvation now required and the savior who reigns related to the topic, "The Myth/Truth of the God Incarnate"? The shifting missional context of these reflections offers a clue. As we move further and further away from the missionary enterprise associated with Euro-American domination of this planet, we find ourselves searching for options to the paternalistic mission of the powerful to the powerless, the patronizing gestures of the wealthy to the poor, the condescending instruction of the enlightened to the benighted. If there was any biblical and theological foundations to the degrading and humiliating gestures of the rescuing missionary who reached out — and above all, reached down — toward the "objects of mission" in the Third World, it was the story of the Incarnation. The story of Jesus as Son of God incarnated in human form to rescue the sinners, represented a model for Christians to follow. They too were to come from above and descend into the depth of other people's problems and rescue them.

Recent biblical scholarship suggests that this reconstruction of the person and work of Jesus is a relatively late formulation which was nurtured on Hellenistic soil outside Palestine.[7] It was but one of several stories which were combined with earlier stories about Jesus to make up a full picture. An earlier Jewish Christian version saw in Jesus a human figure descended from such persons as Adam and David, Eve and Bathsheba. He lived with God in a world dominated by evil forces and brought liberation to people who were possessed or held captive. These Jewish converts did not feel compelled to say with Greek Chris-

---

[7]See for example, Reginald H. Fuller, *The Foundations of New Testament Christology* (London: Lutterworth, 1965), pp. 23-61, 243-50.

tians that Jesus came from God the way other Gentile Christians told the story when they affirmed the divine presence in Jesus. No myth of the Incarnation was necessary.

The important point to notice at the moment is where Jesus began. He started from "down under" and worked from "below," as a human being. The release he brought people was only a foretaste of what was yet to come. So, too, people who see themselves living under domination of manipulators can find in such a story a promise that they too can be avenues of God's liberating actions which will bring deliverance to captives as the reign of God is established.

What is being proposed here follows the classic insight of Christians. We can be like Jesus, but not Jesus in totality. The way they said this was that he was tempted at all points as we are, but without sinning (Hebrew 4:15). In this statement I am saying that we can be like Jesus at some points of the total story which the early Christians established as normative of the redemptive act of human history. But being human we cannot fully reproduce the whole story. We can only relive a portion of it. At one stage of our history some may have been able to live out the incarnational model. Today that model is so inextricably mixed up with the cultural chauvinism, the political manipulations and the economic exploitations of Euro-American civilization and all its devastating consequences, that we need other models of Jesus. The story of the marginalized person working with the overlooked and outmaneuvered holds forth promise. Thus, the rejection of the incarnational model is not based on some metaphysical reasons which are generally invoked, but the weighty considerations of cultural, social and historical settings which have shifted on us. If we do not find appropriate models for this new setting, we will turn the theological heritage into the letter of the law. As stated earlier about Paul, the Law may be "good, just, and spiritual," but if misapplied the word of life can become a sentence of death. Missional action in the face of sin and evil today indicates the impossibility of dehumanizing condescension tied up with the incarnational models and call for the story of one like us who allowed God to be present to bring liberation.

The Following of Jesus and Faith in Christ

Jon Sobrino

My contribution to this conference has no pretensions of being anything other than a presentation of the difficulties, the approaches, and some of the fundamental elements of Christology understood from the perspective of the life and praxis of the Church in Latin America. I shall attempt to show what we believe to be most typical and newest in this way of doing Christology.

The New Challenges of History to Christology

In recent years theologians have treated the understanding and fulfillment of faith in Christ as historical. By historical I mean that faith is disputed and conditioned, but also enabled through history. Faith in Christ cannot emerge on the sidelines of history nor against it. I want in this first section to describe the challenge and the threat of history to the classical tradition of Christology and, more extensively, the suspicions that the classical Christologies create for Latin Americans.

Recent history has been a threat to Christology. This is very clear in the contemporary Christologies coming out of the classical centers of theology. On the one hand, historical research has brought into doubt many of the supposedly historical deeds of Jesus and the transcendental meaning of several of them; examples of these are his miracles, his forgiveness of sins, his consciousness of his divine sonship. On the other hand, the historical process of the West has made the cultural connaturality of the transcendent disappear.

For christological reflection, this has meant the practical impossibility of drawing up a purely descendent Christology starting from transcendence with the key concepts of preexistence and incarnation, whether they originate in dogmatic formulations or neotestamental statements that have commonly been accepted as an expression of that descendent Christology. The historical process of the West has also made the task of finding a continuity between the formulations on the historical Jesus, the postpaschal Christ of the first communities and the Christ of the dogmatic formulations, difficult if not impossible.

Faced with this situation, the reactions have been diverse, including some which are not acceptable from a church point of view; for instance, a Christology without theology or the opposite, a theology without Christology, that is to say, without a binding historical and normative mediation. Positively speaking, a reinterpretation of the very dogmatic, very biblical christological formulas has been attempted in order to rescue the truth of the dogma or of the Scripture and, above all, to rescue their meaning for present-day man. In this latter task there has been help from the different kinds of hermeneutics, which try to show the point from which the formulations about Christ can make sense, be it from a personal, an existential or even a political vantage point. Together with this methodological attempt to place the formulations, there is also a sizable movement that considers it important and even decisive that systematic Christology be based on the historical Jesus.

The common intention of almost all Christologies is a pastoral attempt, albeit carried out scientifically, to make faith in Christ still meaningful and, thus, viable for modern man for whom it is threatened by the new historical and secular consciousness. The crisis to which many of the Christologies speak is fundamentally a crisis of meaning. Present-day history is a threat to the believer, a faith of which until recently he has had peaceful possession. Therefore, in Christology a formal attempt is being made to save the faith threatened by the subjectivity of the believer. The attempt is for modern man — the man who emerges after the Enlightenment, the man who has reached adulthood — to still be able to believe in Christ in some form and to maintain in some way the transcendence of that faith.

This intention is what makes the best present-day Christologies profoundly pastoral. But it should be emphasized that they are directed basically to the individual believer, to the reconciliation between enlightened reason and faith in Christ, to overcoming modern man's sense of being an orphan, either in the Promethean or nihilistic form. So, what is basically behind the modern christological attempts is to respond to the crisis of meaning which a new culture presents.

Given this intention, it is relatively unimportant if the service of Christology to faith in Christ happens through maintaining dogmatic formulations as such or, preferring other more biblical formulations, through starting from the Risen Christ or from the historical Jesus. It is also true that different hermeneutics are used according to the mood and interest of the theologian and the situation which he wants to serve pastorally. But what is important is to respond to the crisis of meaning that history presents to faith in Christ.

In Latin America, in its present historical process, history is a threat for traditional or conventionally progressive Christologies, but in a different sense from that discussed above. Some of the suspicions emerging from historical research and from secularism are also present. The fundamental aspect of the suspicion, however, is not directed at the christological formulations, dogmatic or biblical. And that not only because there is a de facto situation in which the majority of the people are not aware of them nor the majority of theologians make them an explicit object of discussion, but because the suspicion and the crisis to which they have to respond is different. What is suspect is not so much the christological formulations themselves, but rather the use that is being made of them. What is suspect is not so much the "name" of Christ, but what happens and what is done "in the name" of Christ. There is suspicion that Christ has not so much been mythologized as ideologized in order to evade the challenges of history or to cover up its real misery. There is suspicion of a desire to reconcile faith in Christ with enlightened reason and not to reconcile it with objective reality. There is suspicion of a pastoral attempt to rescue the faith of the believer and not to give meaning back to man himself. There is suspicion that Christology is aimed at the nonbeliever or at he whose faith is threatened and is not being aimed at the nonman whose very existence is threatened. These suspicions arise naturally when faced with backward Christologies, but also when faced with other presentations of Christ, apparently more up to date, but which in fact produce a situation where objective reality is abandoned and left to itself. In this sense, any Christology is suspect which presents Christ as a sublime abstraction, as universal reconciliation and, what could appear more shocking, as the absolutely absolute.

If Christ is effectively turned into an abstraction — sublime as it may be — in dogmatic, biblical or theological formulations, and if it is left to the intention of the believer to historify that abstraction, then we run the gravest danger, well confirmed through history, of believing in a Christ who is an extrapolation of determined interests, albeit legitimate ones, much more so when they are illegitimate, egoistic or at least egocentric and oppressive. If Christ is simply the Lord, the Risen One, the Son or, in more systematic formulations, love, power, salvation, then there is the paradoxical danger of being able to manipulate him in the very moment of making a sublime christological confession.

This is the reason why in Latin America so much emphasis is placed on the historical Jesus, despite the obvious difficulties of exegesis. This interest comes not only from the internal difficulties for Christology when it is ignored, but also from that which happens when it is ignored; that is to say, the appropriation by the oppressive system that takes the place of any Christ who is not the historical Jesus. Any kind of abstraction of Christ — however sublime it may be in its formulation, even though it may come about with honest intentions — permitting historifications which leave the door open to injustice or resignation or inaction in the face of it is fundamentally suspect.

If Christ is turned into the ideal of universal reconciliation, then the above suspicions arise again, but in a sharper way in

Latin America. There is no objection to presenting Christian hope christologically from the fullness of Christ, but there is much to object to in the concrete mode of its presentation. The objections stem from two reasons: At a formal level, this presentation of Christ implies presenting him in the final state of his reality, but not in the process of becoming the Christ. The consideration of Christ only at the end of his process or from the end of that process runs the enormous risk of not seeing Jesus *in actu,* that is, in his concrete history and through the process and the ups and downs of that concrete history.

At the level of content the presentation of Christ as reconciliation passes over or excessively softens the conflictive facet of his life and above all his death as a consequence of that conflictive life. It is easily understood that, in a continent like Latin America, Christology cannot be used for reconciliation if a heavy emphasis is not placed on all the conflictive processes through which there can be work for reconciliation. Given the conflictive nature of history, the division and opposition among men as oppressors and oppressed, the injustice and violence generalized, hardened and institutionalized in structures, the reconciliation between men and God and among them in Christ can only be described as a task always to be fulfilled, but not as something already achieved and which can be achieved without passing through the same conflicts through which Jesus passed.

Finally, if Christ is made to represent the absolute from every point of view, there exists the grave danger of disconnecting Christology from real history. It would be an attempt to regionalize and thus make Christology absolute and to ignore the interconnectedness that constitutes Christ himself.

A Christology regionally absolutized, or declared relational only as far as the divine persons are concerned, is a step toward making Christology irrelevant to history and vice versa. Here we find the greatest suspicions, at a logical level of Latin American Christology, that the person of Jesus is discovered only in the depths of his own transcendent relation with the Father and the Spirit; but it is ignored that he is discovered in his concrete bringing about of the Kingdom of the Father.

All these suspicions which coincide at heart in that Christology, even on the basis of generically correct statements, may leave untouched the misery of the historical reality, even when in many present Christologies there is the intention, as we have said, of alleviating the misery of a believer threatened by his faith. It is very good that Christology would make an effort to present Christ in a reasonable way to modern man, but it is unfortunate to forget, in that effort, the humanization of he who is not even a man. It is good to alleviate the feeling of being an orphan, a product of the culture, but it is sad to forget the objective sin of the reality that really makes men orphans. It is good to try to justify the supernatural, but it is wrong to forget the justification of the natural, the bringing of justice to the surrounding historical reality.

It is good to recover the sense of and make explicit the paternity of God, but it would be tragic to forget the real deaths, every day, of the sons of God. It is good, therefore, to work to recover or to find the lost meaning, to overcome the interior loneliness and the threat of being without purpose, to recover the human space that would permit transcendence and to overcome a consequent secularism. But it must not be forgotten that "the worst of the 'secularisms' is the conversion of the sons of God, the temples of the Holy Spirit, the historical Body of Christ, into victims of oppression and injustice, into slaves of economic appetites, into pawns of the political repression" (I. Ellacuria).

We do not want to say that the problematic of meaning for the individual subject who believes in Christ is not present in Latin American Christology. It is present in other forms, is assumed in other ways and has a different meaning for doing Christology. Although the following formulation may sound excessively hard, that which is stated in the Gospel of Mark is also true for Christology: He who wants to save his life will lose it. He who elaborates Christology only for himself, so that "his" faith may have meaning, in order to suffocate doubts and questions, may not achieve that. But he who forgets himself, even when he does Christology, he who does it for the world of the oppressed in order that this world may become more and more like the Kingdom of God, may be pointing to the place and way of life in which faith in Christ may attain full meaning. It may not be a philosophical truth, but it is a Christian truth that in saving others one saves oneself; only saving reality from its nonsense will save the individual subject's own meaning.

According to this, the most profound suspicion is directed toward a Christology which is concerned with the individual, but which forgets objective reality. Furthermore, in Latin America it has become very clear that, strictly speaking, the first task is impossible. Whatever the theological task may be, it has historical repercussions; and it would be an illusion, be it unconsciously or egoistically defended, to say otherwise. Christology as theoretical reflection must adhere to certain conditions which cannot be evaded. It may and should desire to become reflexively conscious of them, but not to eliminate them. Just as theoretical reflection does not enjoy a special status which would permit Christology to go beyond these conditions, and just as these conditions are necessarily historical, Christology will also have to have historical repercussions. In this sense, Christology has a status of external dependence. Because the conditions are not only cultural, but also social, economic and political, its repercussions will extend to all these fields.

Doing Christology, then, also means taking a stand, explicit or implicit, on its own material conditions. It cannot be historically neutral, through action or omission, and must have repercussions in the conflictive interests of history. To ignore these facts would be to mystify the theological discourse and to take sides on the interests of the powerful. On this subject, Latin American theology is quite clear.

A Christology which would not disturb the interests of the powerful because it does not combat them explicitly in the name of Jesus, or because it presents a Christ who is beyond the alternative between oppressors and oppressed, or because it intentionally reduces its problematic to the meaning of the believing individual, would be an ideologized Christology. A Christology which would aim at overcoming antitranscendent secularism without overcoming the type of atheism which hides in injustice, which is no menace to oppressors and does not provoke reaction and persecution against itself, would be highly dangerous. A

Christology which would pretend to be equally for all men and could be worked out equally from the point of view of all men, which would not find its inspiration among the poor of the earth, would also be highly suspicious, since it would inexorably take sides with the status quo. In order to avoid these types of errors, Christology must integrate in its own discourse the real historical conditions and, accordingly, make an option for the type of christological discourse which can better unface the sin of the objective situation and better lead to its defeat according to the Kingdom of God.

A New Theological Method

Latin American theology has argued against Christologies — be they traditional or progressive, dogmatic or biblical, ascending or descending — which have the above-described consequences, and the argument has taken the intuitive form of an "it cannot be so." Far from being superficial, this argument is profound. It is not novel, either. Twenty years ago Karl Rahner argued against a trinitarian theology which was conceptually incomprehensible and salvifically irrelevant. The only difference today is that we repeat the argument not because of Christology's conceptual incomprehensibility, but because it is irrelevant to the transformation of a sinful world into a world according to the Kingdom of God.

Having separated the mediator Jesus from his obvious mediations, obvious generally and historically, such as the radical "no" to the oppression of man by man and the radical "yes" to the building-up of the human family; having separated the mediator Jesus from his own history and personal process, at least in its fundamental characteristics such as discerning the will of a greater God, accepting conflict and the outcome of his historical persecution, and developing his own faith and confidence in the Father; having ignored Jesus' preference for the oppressed of his day; having ignored his call to follow him in announcing and bringing about the Kingdom and in denouncing all sin against the Kingdom — all this forces Latin American Christology to utter an "it cannot be so." In this "no" there come together the experience of daily reality in Latin America and a preliminary grasp of the historical figure of Jesus, even given what little we know of it in detail.

Against this background, Latin American Christology offers an alternative which does not consist principally in perfecting the methods and techniques employed in the various approaches to Christology. Without slighting the perfecting of these methods, it prefers to focus on a new method which offers a thorough alternative. This method obtains in theological reflection in general and therefore also in Christology; but its further theological justification is found in Christology, as we shall see in the last section.

The method of Latin American theology may be described, in general, as reflection on the reality of the faith or as the reflection of the faith become real. This formulation may seem very traditional, but not if one insists on the *becoming real* of the faith. If one thinks, for example, that believing in Christ is simply taking a positive attitude toward biblical or dogmatic texts which offer us a certain content, then we would not call this faith become real. Nor is the conceptual notion of faith superceded by a personalist one — although faith is certainly personal — as if faith simply meant accepting the person of Christ as a fulfilling Thou and a reference point of meaning.

Faith, insofar as it is *Christian* faith, has a different structure which includes the above elements without being identical with them. Christian faith is not a totally autonomous moment within the whole of Christian existence, as if faith once established as such could then require other moments in that existence, like the praxis of charity. We believe that the first thing that Latin American theology did, logically, was to recover the globality of Christian existence within which faith has its own specificity. Throughout history this globality has been expressed in various ways — dogma and ethics; faith, hope and charity; faith and justice. The aim here is not to determine what type of formulation of globality is the most adequate, but merely to insist on the character of the globality. If this is so, then to achieve faith become real is to achieve a kind of Christian existence in which, together with the moment of gift and gratuity, as the moment of meaning, there appears in a fundamental unity the active moment of a doing, whose fundamental direction will be given by the meaning of the faith; but this same meaning goes on becoming real within and not at the edge of the active moment of Christian doing. Therefore, what we understand as reality of the faith is a faith considered not merely in its logical moment of accepting an offered meaning, but rather in its historical moment of practical becoming real, which includes the meaning.

On a general level, this is what we want to assert when we say that Latin American theology is theoretical reflection upon the reality of the faith. And from here one can already see how inadequate a Christology which limits itself to the interpretation of texts about Christ, or to pastoral aids that he might be better understood and accepted will be. This job is important as as one aspect of the theological task, but by itself and without relation to faith become real it is no longer thought of as theology.

Reshaping the faith from day to day is required by the same process of the Spirit of Jesus which continues setting history free. If Latin American theology's emphasis on praxis has philosophical roots in the modern concept of what is knowledge and science, then it also has its roots in the most profound reality of God according to the Christian faith. If the Spirit is not only the one who "will teach us all truth," but "the Lord and giver of life," then giving and shaping life is our way of relating to God in history. One cannot accept God and his son Jesus apart from the Spirit of life and of the concrete life which this Spirit sets free. Only from within the Trinity is God known. But since the "within" of God became a "without" in the Incarnation and in the history which the Spirit continues to set free, only in making life, in pursuing history, in the praxis of the Kingdom, can the mystery of the Father be accepted.

What is vigorously affirmed by Latin American theology are not mere words: "The most progressive theology in Latin America is more interested in *being* liberating than in *talking about* liberation. In other words, liberation belongs not so much to the content but to the method used for doing theology in the face of our reality" (J. L. Segundo). There may be reflection only when there is reality within which one can reflect. There may be liberation theology only from within the effort to really liberate because one will be able to reflect about God, Christ and the Spirit only from within a reality which relates us, certainly in a historical way, to the transcendent reality of God. The new theological method asserts that the path of reflection is the reflection on the historical path shaping the Kingdom of God and toward the fulfillment of this Kingdom.

The Faithful Knowledge of Christ

Fundamentally, to know Christ will basically be a question of affinity and connaturality; he'll be known in the measure in which we go on shaping ourselves like him, doing what he did; he'll be known as the Son in the measure in which we ourselves go on becoming sons. This method does not rule out the difficulty of passing from historical realities and formulations to transcendent ones, but it does point to the place in which the transcendent confession may also arise. Within this process of becoming sons like Christ, we can and must reflect the biblical or dogmatic texts which explicitly express this transcendence.

The fundamental christological epistemology consists, therefore, in the very following of the historical Jesus, that is, in historically recreating the same process of Jesus. For that it is necessary at least to outline the fundamental structure of Jesus' own history and its most essential elements. Without analyzing them in detail, let us at least enumerate those that seem most essential and are most functional in Latin American Christology:

1. the Kingdom of God as absolute reference point of Jesus,
2. Jesus' preference for the poor, and
3. the historical progression of the life of Jesus.

1. The absolute reference point for Jesus is the Kingdom of God. One may catch a glimpse of Jesus's vision through his own prophetic and apocalyptic notions. Above all, however, one grasps it by looking at what Jesus did to serve the Kingdom which was coming. Given the difficulty of determining exegetically the notion which Jesus had of the Kingdom, it's enough to observe Jesus *in actu* serving this Kingdom, that is, the way of life and praxis required by the Kingdom which approaches. This praxis proceeds as the announced good news turns into the good historical reality, and that although Jesus thought that the Kingdom of God is finally grace coming from the same God. The good news works like utopia to guide historical praxis and to make it real.

In this way, the first thing that Jesus puts at the service of the reality of this Kingdom is the denunciation of everything which prevents or destroys the Kingdom; he denounces the sin which turns people into oppressors and oppressed; politically, socially and religiously he uncovers the roots of this sin and unmasks the religious justification of this sin in the divinization of power. Positively, he puts his whole being and all he has into the preaching and praxis of love and justice. His effective solidarity with whoever was oppressed, his activity of curing and exorcising, his proclamation of neighbor love as a main commandment and mediation of the love of God, are all ways in which the good news becomes the good reality.

The vision of God's Kingdom and above all the service *in actu* to this Kingdom are based in Jesus upon an implicit theology of history and of how to make history theologically. From a methodological point of view, the first step in understanding Jesus does not consist, then, in whether there was something especially different in Jesus or not, but in that his own existence is related to the Kingdom of God and thus to the Father — toward a Father who proclaims an unconditional "yes" and an unconditional "no" to human history. Supporting this "yes" and this "no" throughout history is the first and fundamental structure of the life and praxis of Jesus.

2. If the Kingdom of God unifies the praxis of Jesus and the meaning of his own life, then it is important to determine the concrete place of this praxis and its meaning. This place is none other than what we can generally call the world of the poor and oppressed. It's understandable why this fact has been emphasized in Latin America, but being understandable does not lessen its importance for Christology, not as another datum of Jesus'

life, but as a datum which provides the key for understanding him in his human and theological dimension.

It is quite important to emphasize the essential correlation between announcing the good news and announcing it to the poor. Historically, one cannot draw the mission of Jesus from a universal basis, but rather — from the beginning — from a partial one. That the Kingdom of God may include everyone is not in question, but rather that this universality will be achieved only on the basis of the poor. If the privileged recipients of Jesus' mission are the poor, then this supposes a certain perspective on the praxis of the mission, which will render it concrete and, thus, historical and real.

Whatever the personal poverty of Jesus himself, it's clear that his perspective brought him into solidarity with those who may be called the poor and oppressed of his day; this solidarity brought him face to face with a series of historical repercussions for the carrying-out of the mission. Although it has been repeated often, one cannot ignore the visible gestures of solidarity with those in his time who were considered oppressed and outcast, as the evangelists report: the sick, lepers, publicans, women, sinners, Samaritans, and so forth. One must emphasize the consequences of this solidarity. Historically, Jesus' path toward the cross can — and should — be explained on the basis of this solidarity. Jesus' controversies make sense as defense in favor of the oppressed and not just as a discussion of religious casuistry. Jesus unmasks the false religious traditions because it was in their name that people were oppressed. The threats and persecution which run through his life are consequences of the sin of the powerful who felt threatened. The cross and death are the final result of solidarity with the oppressed.

3. The perspective of the poor is also fundamental for understanding the meaning which Jesus attributes to his own life and praxis.

The exercise of the mission is transforming the very person of Jesus. Jesus is forming himself as he shapes the Kingdom of God. The exercise of the mediations of God's will, such as the denunciation of sin, solidarity with the oppressed, the conflicts, the teaching and practice of love and justice, are all transforming the mediator. The generic ideas, attitudes and intentions with which Jesus begins his mission become concrete in the course of his life process and thus transform his very self.

We are not trying to psychologically analyze Jesus' subjectivity, for which there is little evidence in the Gospels; but we do want to say two important things: the existence of process in the life of Jesus and the fundamental correlation between objective historical praxis toward the Kingdom and subjective attitude toward God.

As difficult as it may be to establish Jesus' biography or even a chronology of his life, it seems sufficiently clear that in his outward activity there are various stages crossed by what has come to be called the Galilean crisis. The prayer in the garden does not manifest the same experience of God as the elated prayer of thanksgiving. The expectation of the Kingdom's early arrival gives way to uncertainty. His readiness to contribute to the Kingdom progresses from the submission of his qualities and work to the submission of his own life. Sin will no longer just be something which must be denounced, but something which must be borne.

As difficult as it may be to analyze the concrete process of Jesus' life, the Gospel narratives agree that such a process, in which Jesus is transforming himself in a certain way, exists. In this transformation it is very important to note, at least in a systematic way, the correlation between outward activity and inward attitude. The kind of inward processes, of which the Gospels give some hint, are initiated as well as made possible by his praxis. The temptations, understood not only as isolated events but also as the climate in which his life unfolds, are produced by his search for the messianic approach to building the Kingdom. His ignorance or uncertainty hinge upon how and when the Kingdom will come. His fidelity to the Father is made possible by his fidelity to history, when the latter buffets him with threats and persecution. This inward and outward process is what shapes Jesus. In his historical praxis may be found those elements which make his interiority possible, so that the meaning of God as "Father" may have real weight, and there may also be found those elements which prevent this attitude from being naive and idealist, but rather dialectical in the fact of historical crises.

Getting to know Jesus in the described manner, at least in its fundamental structures, would not be more than working out a more or less correct Jesusology. But this would not be a Christology, that is, the reflection that Jesus is the Christ and that the practice of Jesus is fundamentally normative. To take this second step, Latin American theology has insisted upon the following of Jesus, that is, that we recreate the basic structures of Jesus' life in the explained manner, and that at the level of historical as much as theological structures.

Latin American Christology has not made its greatest effort in showing that Jesus is the Christ because he is different from other alleged christs, but in first showing the possibility of really knowing Jesus so that then one may confess him as the Christ. It's not a matter of methodologically doubting that Jesus is the Christ, but rather of being more aware of the content of what being Christ concretely means and of how to come to know him.

The possibility of this real knowledge is found in following him in discipleship. Coming to believe is made possible by a praxis of building the Kingdom: but what one must believe also points to the global meaning of existence and of history. Latin American theology emphasizes that grasping this meaning is finally not a matter of an arbitrary decision or even of a reasonable decision, but rather of this meaning becoming historically and practically real. Thus, to believe in Christ will be possible to the extent in which one can come to believe as Christ. In him we recognize meaning for our own life insofar as our own makes sense living as he lived. In this manner the following of Jesus will be *a priori* the way of approaching the object of Christology.

In Jesus' own life he himself suggested the meaning of getting in touch with him, of knowing him, beginning with the call to discipleship. This call to discipleship also has its own history, depending on what phase of his life Jesus was in. In the first stage of his life, following Jesus means working on the same mission as he does, announcing the Kingdom of God and making it real. In the second stage, the required discipleship puts more emphasis on undergoing the same process as he does. In any case, it's not a matter of a pious imitation or reduction, but rather of recreating the same structure of Jesus' process.

In order to proceed from Jesusology to Christology, it is very important from the start to remember that Jesus calls others to follow him. This call is not just one more thing that he does in his life, but something fundamental to his own activity and so for knowing him personally. Logically it could have been different. The Christ did not have to request discipleship, he could have conceived the mission in another way, so that all others were only its recipients. But this logical arrangement did not take place. The real Christ called people to share his mission. And thus it belongs essentially to the very person of Christ to be one who calls. And thus Jesus is not simply there to be accepted or rejected as the Christ, but is there to be followed or merely beheld. Strictly speaking, there cannot be a rejection of Christ apart from discipleship, since there is no other way of knowing what Christ we are talking about. This means that people can decide to follow Jesus or not, from within this discipleship they can carry on or quit, but apart from such discipleship they won't know which Jesus is at stake. Thus becoming Jesus' follower is indispensable for knowing Jesus.

To know Jesus and to know the meaning of his own life, one must be ready for discipleship. This is congruent with the trinitarian reality of God. Theologically, the reality of Jesus is relational with respect to the Father and, historically, this relationship is expressed toward the Kingdom of God. To know Jesus, then, is nothing else but to introduce ourselves into this relationship. To want to know Jesus directly, to want to affirm or deny his being Christ solely on the basis of his own person, is an attempt condemned to fail. We will know Jesus as the Son in the measure in which our own life is a life of sonship. Latin American Christology tries to reflect on Christ from within the praxis of becoming historically like him; it tries to reflect on his sonship from within the becoming real of the sonship of all people.

Then, is Jesus really the Christ? Latin American Christology is not usually in the habit of either asking this question explicitly or of answering it argumentatively. The *fact* of faith in Christ poses it from within discipleship. If one accepts and makes real that Jesus' way is the correct way toward the Kingdom of God and toward the God of the Kingdom, then one is admitting that Jesus is the Christ. The correctness of this faith flows from its real consequences rather than from *a priori* arguments about the uniqueness of Jesus or his possible self-consciousness or his miraculous powers. Not that these themes are not taken up, but not taken up as the fundamental and independent manner of reasoning about Christ. The correctness of this faith verifies itself if following Jesus truly makes a person more human, better displays the correlation between the *gloria Dei, vivens homo* or, more concretely, between the *gloria Dei, vivens pauper.* Argumentatively, perhaps one cannot say much more about Christ.

It is understandable why the fundamental problem of Latin American Christology is not the biblical or dogmatic formulations concerning Christ, considered in themselves. Nor will the solution to this problem be found by ignoring these formulas or by reinterpreting them or selectively choosing those which are culturally more attractive. Naturally, these formulas are analyzed and new ones developed — such as Jesus the liberator. But these formulas are not in and of themselves independent, privileged sources of christological knowledge, even if they are necessary so that the path of discipleship may have a first generic direction. The true source of christological knowledge is the following of Christ become real, within which the formulations are understood as doxological affirmations. In them is expressed the transcendent meaning of what is transcendent in the history of discipleship.

Latin American Christology tries to reflect on the primordial unity which exists between the following of Jesus as contemporary historical reality and the Jesus who calls to discipleship. To grasp this primordial unity is the most typical feature of Latin American Christology. Thus, this type of Christology neither thinks of itself as only a service to elucidate christological formulas, as if concrete history only made sense by ending in a formulation of faith, nor does it think of itself only as at the service of history, as if christological formulas ought to be directed exclusively toward historical efficacy. Latin American Christology strives, rather, for the unity of both things, and the history of Latin American Christology is nothing but the history of dialectically relating both dimensions.

*   *   *

By a tragic coincidence, as I finished writing these reflections a new dramatic event occurred in El Salvador. About forty young people — ranging in age from twelve to twenty years — who were taking part in an introductory Christian weekend, were sleeping peacefully in a retreat house. At six in the morning, some security agents who arrived in tanks entered the building and, in cold blood, killed the priest Octavio Ortiz and four of the young people. He is the fourth priest killed in less than two years, and there are hundreds of other Christians who have been murdered, imprisoned, tortured, and who have disappeared.

These facts best explain what I have tried to say about the meaning of faith in Christ. These martyrs are real witnesses of the faith, who teach us in truth what believing in Christ means. By following him, by announcing the good news to the poor, by being in solidarity with them, by struggling for their just causes, many Christians in El Salvador and other countries in Latin America try to live like Jesus, are persecuted like Jesus and die like Jesus. The reflections of Latin American Christology take life from these lives. They are the hermeneutical place for understanding Christ.